Caregiving

Caregiving

MY STORY, YOUR GUIDE

OLIVER J. DESOFI

ARPress
ILLUMINATING IDEAS.
EMPOWERING VOICES

ARPress
45 Dan Road Suite 36
Canton MA 02021

Hotline: 1(800) 220-7660
Fax: 1(855) 752-6001

Ordering Information:
Quantity Sales. Special discounts are available on quantity purchases by corporations, associations, and others. For details, contact the publisher at the address above.

Printed in the United States of America.

ISBN-13   Paperback   979-8-89389-733-3
               eBook   979-8-89389-734-0

Library of Congress Control Number: 2024922221

Table of Contents

Foreword

This book is about my personal experience of being a Caregiver...how I became one, everything I learned along the way and what a wonderful life two people can have together regardless of the situation. More can be learned about this author by going to www.desofibook.com which also features my autobiography titled "Intrigue, Capitalism, Love:–My True Story"

This book is dedicated to the memory of my wife who succumbed in September 2010 after a long battle with Multiple Sclerosis. My wife had the severest form of this incurable disease. As a Caregiver to her I have learned much and I want to share it with as many people as possible – information from doctors and insurance companies to positive thinking and a happy life.

While my personal stories relate directly to my wife, MS and our life, all of the information I share directly relates to all Caregivers and, unfortunately, many situations – from disease to disabled veterans.

This is not meant to be a biography; it is truly about Caregiving – from beginning to middle...never "end". It is a unique and documented description about the evolution of a severely disabling disease. At the same time it shows the important and growing Caregiver expertise to maintain a stable balance between patient and Caregiver.

While I believe a positive attitude is vital, there are statements in this book that appear as negative. My goal is to make you aware of different situations from my experiences and research including the negative ones that you might encounter. I will cover insurance and pharmaceutical companies, medical professionals, etc. I am not implying that all of them are bad. I just want to make you aware of certain situations or conditions and hopefully this book will help keep that negativity from you.

Awareness can truly lead to making life easier for both the patient and the Caregiver…after all, if you can learn from just reading about it and thus avoiding potential problems, then it will make your lives more simple and positive.

Someone else's knowledge about something negative can make things more positive for you…and that is an important part of what this book is about.

We all wish to never face trying situations such as those described, but if that is not preventable, I truly hope the knowledge shared with you will create an uplifting and helpful experience.

Is this book different as compared to others with similar titles? This book is based on real life experiences, not a collection of ideas put together by individuals who have not been "battle" tested in the totality of Caregiving. It doesn't mean that those books are not valuable, but I view them more like the yellow pages. They usually are a wonderful collection of data compiled from the internet and government sources and provide answers to many general issues. Some of the literature concentrates more on potential legal requirements and others on broad statistical data leading to flawed conclusions and recommendations. Many of the "must do" issues are not practical or truly useful in real life.

The approach of this book is to guide and mold your attitude toward a very intriguing, involved and complicated job. It doesn't necessarily mean that the Caregiving job must be all or nothing, but even if you are involved in just pieces of the total job, your attitude, managerial, organizational and psychological skills are constantly being tested and fine tuned. This book describes how one caregiver, over a period of 24 years, was able to maneuver across the battlefield, still survive and not succumb to battle fatigue. This book is not an instruction manual because of the huge variety of conditions it would have to cover. Attempting such a job would entail an effort which in the end would exceed all the information covered in our tax code and that is a mouthful.

My Wife's Views and Experiences

(Dictated to a dear friend.)

While I am almost totally bed-ridden as a result of a debilitating disease, which has robbed me of my abilities to do almost anything, I am at peace.

My loving husband, who I trust implicitly, gives me that peace of mind. He is always around and I don't worry about anything, I mean anything! I can be frustrated, depressed or irritated and use him as my outlet to express my emotions because I know he will never get upset and he will lift my spirits with a smile and a joke. Sometimes I feel he has strange powers to make me forget a pain or even make it disappear. He places his hand on my head and it appears to have a healing effect, it is strange. Any frustration or depression begins to evaporate.

I used to be a very independent person and had no problems understanding situations before my eyes and make decisions instantly. My disease has impacted my ability to visualize things now, but my husband has stepped in and taken over. In so doing, while I am on my back, he has managed to still make me feel like I am in control and his participating partner. He makes me feel like nothing has changed. Here is a very specific example. Today, the day of our wedding anniversary, he went shopping. When he came home, he opened a package and expressed his delight for the gift I had just bought him for our anniversary. He said, "I know that if you would have been with me and I admired this item, you would buy it and say this is my gift to you for our anniversary." He is right. He knows how I think and he makes me feel like I am still his participating partner.

When he lifts me out of the bed and places me into the wheelchair because we have to go out, either to a restaurant, the doctor or to visit someone, he makes sure I always wear a beautiful dress. He searches through catalogs to find the type of dress I would pick, something unique and colorful, some garment that just looks great. He takes great care to make me feel good about myself. His biggest reward is when someone makes the comment, "You look so great," which makes him laugh, because he knows how much I hate that expression ever since we went through the Social Security Disability nightmare.

When I go to sleep, I thank GOD every night that He brought this affectionate and loving person into my life and to have me share it with him.

I am the luckiest person! (Dictated on November 20, 2006)

Introduction

When your father, mother, husband, wife, son or daughter gets a high fever or a cold – for only the next three days – you take care of them – chicken soup, tea with lemon and honey, orange juice, sponge bath, aspirin – whatever is needed for the person you love – you give them all of this and especially caring and love – and hope they get better.

For temporary disabilities or more severe impairments we usually rely on the medical profession and the general health care environment to restore us to the condition before the impairment. This temporary departure from what we consider to be normal is generally covered, at least to a degree, by health insurance.

The picture changes drastically when the disability or impairment becomes permanent. This is true of the person in this book and thousands of people that are loved and need to be CARED for 24/7 – all year long. Some things just last longer than a cold – but EVERYTHING can be OVERCOME to create an enriched life and environment even under those conditions.

It's the love that counts...combined with some knowledge to make things as rewarding as possible! Don't ever give up – find an answer...if you can't find a clinical answer, keep searching for the emotional answer.

Caregiving

"Caregiving" is provided to a person, who for whatever reason has become disabled and cannot, as a result of such impairment; perform functions normally done automatically without spending a minute thinking about it.

We all know – and of course don't want to accept – that when we get older there will be physical limitations on our lives. Hopefully, the kinds we can deal with such as…it hurts to pick up the paper but a neighbor brings it in every morning or you can't always drive but someone will hopefully be around to take you shopping or to doctors appointments and yet, with all of this, you manage to take care of the rose garden. With old age, you prepare in advance as much as possible, hope for the best and truly enjoy the things you can.

Then there are times when you are unfortunately stricken with a disabling disease, a victim of an accident or a disabled veteran…no one prepares for this… EVER… including a potential Caregiver – no preparation!

So, before we go into Caregiving, here's the important question for the patient/victim (and of course, a potential Caregiver).

Should you be totally disabled and you would be free to select one of the two options listed, which would be your preference?

Choice 1 – Enter a nursing home or assisted living facility
or
Choice 2 – Stay at home and have a Caregiver support you.

If you selected choice 1, do you have the financial resources or insurance which will give you the ability to select the very best? If the answer is YES, that is wonderful, but you happen to be in the minority. If the answer is NO, do you really want to be cared for by an institution which cannot afford to get the best and higher paid individuals? You may be guided by the fact that if you are unable to pay, that Social Services will come to the rescue and give you some support. But the question was which one would be your preference, not which one would you have to accept, no matter what.

If you picked choice 2, you picked the one preferred by the majority. If you are fortunate to have a dedicated family member volunteer for the job out of sheer love and without any compensation, also hoping that somehow you end up with some disability income, you are extremely fortunate. Your financial resources will dictate the support you may qualify for. Currently the very poor, those that have minimal income and hardly any assets will probably receive the most comprehensive support. Those still referred to as the "Middle Class," are facing the most difficult obstacles. They are not poor enough to qualify for assistance because they are considered to be too RICH. They are really between the rock and the hard place. Their financial resources don't allow them to fund the extensive support required to sustain a severally disabled person for a prolonged period of time. Unless our Health Care environment sees some drastic changes, this group of people will join the poorest in our country at a steep cost to the taxpayer. Then you have the real "Upper Income People" who, because of their financial status, are rarely even interested in becoming caregivers. They are more interested in pawning their disabled family members off to someone …anyone or an institution. Those individuals are usually to busy playing golf, can't be bothered for whatever reason and are greedy to top it off. They like to negotiate the lowest payment possible for any of the many services available. Some of them like to disconnect their phones so that an institution can't even ask them a question, after all, if they pay whatever has been agreed to and the check shows up like clockwork, they contend that they have done their duty. Some rare exceptions can be found in this group. There are some charities which will give some support, provided you qualify based on whatever rules guide them.

The majority of people questioned about their choice for Caregiving prefer to stay at home and be taken care of in a familiar environment. While it is less costly than a nursing home or an assisted living facility, it requires an understanding of the totality of the Caregiving job.

I can describe the totality because I decided to give up a career when I had reached the top and retired early from my job as a corporate CEO to honor the vow of marriage and become a 24/7 caregiver for my wife. I have stayed by her side for the last 24 years and have assumed ALL the duties of a caregiver. This story is not intended to insinuate or portray the job of caregivers as an ALL or NOTHING type job. The degree of Caregiving that an individual wants or can take on is a very personal matter and depends on the individual's mental readiness, physical capability, passion, commitment and dedication to an extremely complex job. Specific financial capability obviously plays a major role and can make a big difference.

One has to understand that the fictitious advertisement I answered (**see Appendix B**), specifically "keeping loads of records, long hours, no pay, no benefits, no bonus, no vacation, no coffee breaks, meals on the run and willing to work in any environment" and YES, "sometimes be the recipient of abuse," could be very real.

Let's take a look at the job of a "Caregiver." Ironically there are no universities, colleges or trade schools which prepare people for the most complex and involved jobs, like the "Homemaker" or "Caregiver".

The "Mother/Father" profession receives some training or direction before the baby is born but "pretty much it is on the job training" after birth. While there are guides for parents, no such guide is available for one of the most complex jobs, the Caregiver. These skills can only be learned through "on the job training." Individuals who take this job seriously and fully dedicate themselves in order to excel to perfection will be more skilled than those who graduate from a college and are able to show off a framed diploma for their achievements. Corporations seem to be inclined to rate the diploma holding individual higher than the "on the job trained" individual. How ironic! The vast majority of people would look at the "Caregiver" job not as a highly skilled profession but with a feeling of sorrow for the poor soul. In their view "Caregivers" are probably rated below "Homemakers." It is a fact that the "Homemaker" job is usually portrayed in a demeaning fashion. So let's put the "Caregiver" job on the map. A talented "Caregiver" would make a better CEO for any major corporation than those currently in office and being rewarded with multimillion dollar bonuses.

The multitudes of issues facing a corporate executive are no different than those faced by the CEO of "his/her" Caregiver organization. As a Caregiver you must make life saving decisions. You be the judge – MONEY vs THE LIFE OF A LOVED ONE. Money can be lost and regained, once a life is lost, it cannot be regained. So which job carries a heavier burden and which job should be valued higher?" Certainly not the corporate CEO! For those who will show utter contempt for this statement, allow me to give you the rebuttal. I can make this statement based on my personal knowledge, since I was a corporate CEO before accepting the promotion to Caregiver.

There is no doubt that many non-Caregiver CEO's spend more then 40 hours per week on the job but never 24/7. The caregiver job without exception is 24/7 unless additional people get involved or the patient is admitted to an institution.

For those 24/7 caregivers being able to overcome and coping with the stress created by this type of a schedule is called "multitasking." The ability to meticulously schedule and plan is extremely important to the Caregivers mental health. Ironically, whenever we undertake anything, we certainly don't plan to fail, but how frequently do we fail to plan? Events have to be scheduled in such a way that they contribute to the Caregiving chore, while at the same time giving the Caregiver short bursts of time to do something enjoyable to them.

Those that are 24/7 Caregivers will tend to agree with this analysis. So what are the requirements for a skilled and top-notch Caregiver?

- professional manager who also posses some psychological skills
- medical professional in a variety of specialties but only covering a segment of that specialty
- dietician
- skilled nurse in regard to the patients specific requirements
- nurse's aide
- pharmacist
- financial wizard
- insurance and tax specialist

- skilled observer, research analyst and be able to correlate and interpret patient symptoms
- must be able to represent the patient forcefully and cannot be timid
- tremendous patience and compassion

In general, people seem to see a Caregiver as a person who is somewhat like a nurse. This couldn't be further from the truth. Caregiving relates with a patient in a very unique relationship.

Taking care of a spouse (or any loved one) invariably results in a major change in lifestyle. It is one you have to accept as a Caregiver – period – if not – find someone else for the job! A Caregiver has to realize that their own life has changed as well in supporting the person they love…and it absolutely does not mean bringing down the quality of your own life.

The Caregiver who responds to a sudden change in status, from being a "normal" person to Caregiver of a totally disabled person, has to be a fast learner. If financial resources are available, as a result of insurance or inherent wealth, the Caregiver will acquire those resources in order to perform the totality of the job.

If those financial resources, whatever they may be, are not readily available, the afflicted party will suffer the consequences. The Caregiver will be unprepared and cannot fill the gap in required knowledge by hiring the expertise to bring the lifestyle of the patient into an area of acceptability.

A Caregiving responsibility is one of evolution and is tightly related to the patient being taken care of. How this relationship evolves is the key to being a successful Caregiver, one who will have a patient with a positive outlook, a superior mindset and who will become an active contributor to their own longevity.

The first task, after recognizing or accepting the diagnosis of MS (and other diseases as they relate), is the fact that currently there is no possible reversal to the slow downward progression of the disease. The first casualty is our pre-conceived notion that we are sick and will get better. The person who moves from healthy to quadriplegic in a very brief moment has no choice but to accept the condition imposed on him or her. The slow and multi-year downward transition creates a mindset which initially, due to its non-acceptance, is setting the stage for more serious problems later as the disease follows its non reversible course.

MS people experience remissions, more so in the earlier years, less in subsequent years and usually none many years later. Remissions are interpreted by many MS afflicted people as "I am either getting better" or "I beat this thing called MS and I am OK" or the whole idea is just plainly swept under the rug. If you view remissions in that vein, you are setting the stage for more unpleasant surprises which have nothing to do with the disease. Many are environmental. Ask yourself: Where do you live, do you live in a house with steps, does your handwriting suffer, are you afraid of stepping on a ladder because you may fall? Not so long ago you had the ability to keep a perfect balance but now you don't want to be viewed as a complainer.

Well, when you are diagnosed with MS or any other non-curable disease, you and your Caregiver, usually someone very close to you such as your parents, your spouse, sisters and brothers or even your children, should start planning together for what will be the inevitable result of your disease.

As early as possible you should plan for your future living quarters. They should be wheelchair accessible, even if you are not in a wheelchair yet. Your living quarters shouldn't have any steps, any sliders should have the rails recessed and flush to the ground, doors should be at least three feet wide, all of them. Bathrooms should accommodate wheelchairs and should be wide enough so that you can easily turn. You should not have a tub, but a roll-in. You should have bars installed so that the patient, at least in the initial stages, still can hold on in order to lift themselves out of the chair. Some counters and kitchen accessories should be lower for easier access. At this mid-range of disability, the Caregiver is supportive when required. Basically he or she is more of an assistant or associate. It is a difficult role because the patient wants to do as much as possible. They want to feel useful while the Caregiver wants to help to make life easier for the patient. This in itself will cause conflicts. Patients will have a tendency to express their feelings by saying, "Hey, let me do this, I am not disabled," forcing the Caregiver to back off without getting annoyed or insulted. When the patient has transitioned to the final stage of almost being quadriplegic, the Caregiver now becomes totally dedicated to just monitor and extend the life of the patient.

To be successful, this phase of the relationship building becomes one of the most important in the life of both. Here the relationship with the spouse (or anyone else) is the key to long term success.

Unfortunately, a very high percentage of MS afflicted people are abandoned by their healthy spouse. There are a number of stated reasons for this, but the true underlying problem allowing this to happen is the lack of building very close and understanding relationships with the afflicted partner. In the earlier years it should be the goal of the couple to do as many things as humanly possible before it will become impossible. What to do depends on your likes and dislikes but probably the best approach would be to view what you as couples have talked about regarding your retirement plans. Think of doing it now or as close to now as possible. It will also strengthen your relationship. My wife and I did and it was the best time of our lives. For some strange reason, the ones that do the "abandoning" would probably be the biggest complainers if the situation were reversed. There are words for it. The words are "selfish or self-centered." I have heard that after the death of the spouse, who was the patient, the Caregiver's advice was, "Don't ever become a Caregiver – it robs you of your precious time." Strange advice! If your time is more precious than your loved one's comfort and well-being then I say, "It is sound advice – I just hope the individual will find comfort on the trip to the final resting place upon entering the elevator at the end of their life, when he or she only finds the DOWN button in working order."

The documented description of our 49 year experience as patient/Caregiver from a perfectly mobile and generally healthy person (the patient) to a quadriplegic state is described as it really happened and is a rare insight for any person afflicted by a progressive and ever debilitating disease. If you ask your neurologist about the potential course of the MS progression or any other non-curable disease, he or she will tell you, it is impossible to predict and there are no specific patterns.

Our joint progression will give you a very good idea. The expert Caregiver role evolved as a result of a love story which brought the patient and Caregiver together in such a way that when the patient had to let go of whatever was no longer possible to do, the Caregiver jumped in and picked up the function.

As a result of the Caregiver evolution one cannot write a book which describes in detail what the responsibilities of a Caregiver are – they change almost daily.

Adaptation to change probably has to be one of the primary attributes and assets of any person who will be a Caregiver for a patient who loses their capabilities over a prolonged period of time.

It is also very important to realize that becoming a disabled person is not by choice and it certainly isn't something that may only happen to someone else. IT CAN HAPPEN TO ANYONE AT ANY TIME, therefore this book could become a description of your own life. No matter which side of the fence you may be positioned, patient or Caregiver, the probability that during your lifetime you will escape from all parts of what is described, is minuscule.

My wife is suffering from the worst of the different versions of Multiple Sclerosis. She has primary progressive MS and has now been suffering from the consequences of this disease for 49 years. What are the consequences? To a perfectly healthy person and unaware of the plight of disabled people, the following description may sound quite depressing. This is not intended to make you feel depressed. It is intended to put this disease in the proper context and to show, how even under the most adverse conditions, love can't conquer all, but it certainly can achieve quite a bit and sure make Life Worth Living!

At this point, my wife has reached a quadriplegic state. On a scale from 1 to 10, one (1) being at the low end of "bad" and ten (10) at the high end of "really bad", physically she is rated a nine (9). How did we get to this point?

The pages that follow are written in a biographical style in order to properly portray the evolution of one person's illness and WHEN, HOW and WHY a Caregiver evolved.

You will find descriptions which on the surface may appear to be unrelated to the patient's disease or could be interpreted as non Caregiver issues. To put it in the proper context, it is important to understand that many actions had a research element attached to it.

I realized early on that we, both of us, were dealing with a mystery, much more involved and complicated. Before the patient, specifically my wife, was diagnosed, we tried a myriad of approaches and documented the results. We were determined, to the best of our ability, avoid mistakes and misinterpretations. The future is always a surprise. Proper planning and interpretations will increase the probability that the outcome will be favorable. Since the beginning of my wife's disease, major milestones have been achieved by the medical researchers and new tools have become available to diagnose ailments faster and better, but in spite of it, it has not diminished the discovery of ever more mysterious ailments.

The analytical concepts used during the evolutionary progression of my wife's disease will still be valid but in the future will have to deal with new medical mysteries.

Due to the totally unrecognized symptoms which affected my wife's life, we needed to stay focused and not be sidetracked by remissions, an expression unknown to anyone at that time, something which could potentially prompt my wife to make erroneous or damaging decisions affecting her future health. A simply example of what I mean is many people love to sunbath, my wife did too. Before she was diagnosed with MS we had no idea that extended sun exposure and high humidity would have some very unusual and more severe fatigue factors associated with it. Now we know better.

Try to remember there always was a specific meaning behind all the actions, all intended to extend the life of the patient in the most enjoyable way. It is also written with the intent to allow you to make some gross and broad comparisons, like "how does my timeline and situation compare to the described evolutionary experience." As broad as it may be, it is better than nothing. I also want to state again that one of the objectives always was and still is to make sure that my wife will never reach the point which would prompt her to say the most dreaded sentence, "I wish I were dead!"

What Happened Along the Way

The highlights of the 49 year documented bumpy ride of a patient from a perfectly functioning person to a quadriplegic state and the concurrent evolution of a Caregiver from neophyte to expert.

YEAR	PATIENT EVENT	CAREGIVER–CHALLENGE
		Before Diagnosis
1	The beginning	NONE.
2	Strange syndromes	Perplexed
4	Minor accidents	Can't be normal
5	Parents inattention	Relationship development
6	Why see Neurologist-feel fine!	Not optimistic-Neurologist not helpful
8	Problems disappeared, for good?	Falling in love with patient
9	Syndromes reappear	What is going on-Doctors clueless
10	No problems-cured?	False sense of security
11	Potential serious accident	Accident prevented-Caregiver marries patient
12	Another accident	Frustrated with medical profession
13	No longer employed	Increased attention-mindset boosters
15	Overconfident-last attempt at skiing	Roller coaster ride continues
16	Giving birth-increase in syndromes	Bottom of the class doctors?
19	Slower reaction time-driving impacted	Answer-Off Road Vehicle (Jeep)
20	Daughter's accident-more problems	Adrenaline rush

After Diagnosis

21	Finally DIAGNOSIS-in denial	Top of the class doctor!
22	Needs a cane	
24	Must move-Handicap friendly home	Must retire early
25	NO INSURANCE for MS	More intervention and help
27	Apply for disability	Success!
28	Motorized scooter	100% dedication-relationship stronger
29	Fulfilling dream	Motor home not beneficial
31	High degree of spasticity	New power wheelchair required
32	Country demeaning to the disabled	Saudi Arabian adventure?
33	Now goes the bladder	New Caregiving environment
34	Role reversal-consoling caregiver	Emotionally difficult period
39	Dentist experience	On guard! Protect patient from scams
40	Emergency Room	Beware of do-gooders!
41	Nerve pain and catheter problems	Major decision-potentially life prolonging
42	Nerve pain and Neurontin	Decisions-Decisions!
43	Can't feed herself any longer	One more for list of "things to do"
44	New treatment plan?	Not appropriate. Turning it down
45	The Central American research project	Risky approach
46	The worst year ever-close to death	True 24/7 Caregiving-Stress at its peak
47	Slow recovery-Eliminate catheter	Mostly taking over from doctors
48	Greatly improved-better than 2 yrs ago	The greatest reward
49	Improvements wiped out	Professional failures!

YEAR 1:
Patient: The beginning.
Observations: NONE.

The first time I ever laid my eyes on my future wife was when she came in for an interview in the early part of 1960. At that time I was working for American Airlines as an analyst for the new computer organization, called SABRE, the name which became known as the famous airline reservation system, the first real-time commercial system in the world. She was a beautiful petite lady and looked like a million bucks. I was praying that the technical manager who needed a secretary would select her and he did.

The doctor who finally diagnosed her Multiple Sclerosis in 1980 estimated that she had contracted it when she was 19 years old. Well, when she joined American Airlines, she was one month short of 19. Did she have MS at that time or did she get it after she joined? Based on stories of "clumsiness" when she was younger, I believe she either was born with it or got it years before age 19.

As I said before, the disease was not diagnosed until 1980. We had no idea why my future wife was having these strange symptoms, however for the sake of clarity and in order to make comments along the way regarding MS, sometimes I will describe things as if we knew about the disease before 1980.

YEAR 2:
Patient: Strange syndromes.
Observations: Perplexed.

One year after she joined American Airlines, the company transferred us to a new office location and she became my secretary. As time passed we had many conversations regarding her losing balance, running into door frames, dropping things and the tingly (pins-and-needles) feeling that usually occurred on her left side. Each time we talked about it, she always told me her father was quite unkind and called her names, all coupled with "clumsy".

Since I had my own two children from a previous marriage, I found that behavior by her father quite strange. I really didn't focus on it until a year and half later, the middle of 1963, when my son was suddenly diagnosed with child diabetes. I noticed a behavior problem within a week and took him to the doctor. The doctor was quite complimentary that I had brought him in immediately and as a result was able to control his diabetes from inception without a major problem.

While having a sandwich in my office for lunch my secretary and future wife came in and wanted to know if she could join me and eat her lunch in my office. I waved her in. Of course, I had no objections.

Earlier I had overheard conversations between her and another employee regarding her bow and arrow fishing episodes. I asked her, "What was that all about?" She explained that she had gotten a New York Croton Aqueduct license for bow and arrow fishing. I was intrigued by that sport, because it requires some mathematical precision to hit a fish under water with an arrow. The reflection plus the water surface creates an optical illusion making the fish appear in a different location than where it really is and that must be taken into account when aiming. I couldn't reconcile this ability in light of her father's contention that she was so clumsy. Being a hunter myself, I know if you are a clumsy hunter, the chances of being very successful at this, or any other sport, is highly unlikely.

The reason this particular episode was so meaningful to me was because as we found out later, she already had Multiple Sclerosis. At different times she was telling me how she would lose her balance for no apparent reason. She also had noticed that her walking was difficult sometimes and she became excessively exhausted while other times she would be OK. She told me about an episode when she was walking home from school and while crossing a street, her left leg suddenly caved in and she fell. I asked if her parents ever took her to a doctor to find out why she had these occurrences. She said, "No."

I encouraged her to see a neurologist. She did and unfortunately, the diagnosis at that time was – "It's all in your head, there is nothing wrong." In the early 60's, diagnosing Multiple Sclerosis apparently had not been invented yet. In the meantime, occasionally she would have an auto accident. She could never pinpoint the reason for it–it just happened. I told her that just does not sound right, things don't just happen for no apparent reason. You must have some underlying medical problem. Since I am a very analytical person, I took a lot of interest in her situation and asked her many questions to see if I could figure out what the problem was. Each time I did, she just said that I was a pain in the ass. I still was undeterred and as I got to understand her more and more, my affection and interest for her also grew. She knew what happened to my son Dean and I told her that as a result of that experience I was very sensitive to things like that.

YEAR 4:
Patient: Minor accidents.
Observations: Can't be normal.

She loved to ski and as winter approached she would drive to New Hampshire where she was a member of a ski lodge. I remember the Monday morning after her return from one of those trips. She and I arrived at the computer center parking lot at the same time. Several weeks before she had bought a brand new "Malibu," it was a beautiful car. I noticed quite a dent over the right front wheel. After I parked, I waited for her and asked her what had happened. She said, she ran off the road and hit a guardrail. Since it was cold, she said, "I tell you what, invite me to lunch and I'll explain the whole event." I had to laugh and said, "You sure don't miss an opportunity to get a free lunch, it's a deal." About 11:30AM, I took her to lunch. After we ordered our food, I asked her to tell me exactly what had happened. She had left for New Hampshire after work on Friday. The ski lodge was located somewhere between Lake Winnipesaukee and the White Mountain ski area. That's a 300 mile drive and took her about five and half hours. I made the comment, "that's going pretty fast." Her response, "this time I didn't get a speeding ticket." Anyhow, she described the whole weekend and said that again she fatigued more than she thought she should. She left on Sunday morning around eleven to return home. I asked her if she had been drinking or if she went to sleep too late. She assured me she went to sleep around ten, because she was really exhausted and never had any booze. On her way home, after about a three hour drive, in a slight bend of the road, she suddenly hit the curb, jumped it and scraped the guard rail. She stopped immediately and was all shook up because she never noticed any drifting toward the right. After she calmed down, she continued on her homebound trip. She then explained that just a few weeks before this incidence, she had gone skiing to the Adirondacks with her brother and sister-in-law. She had fallen several times for no reason whatsoever. Her knees just buckled and she couldn't figure out why that would happen. The terrain was normal and she never had that experience before.

After we had lunch, we walked to the restaurant parking lot and I gave her the keys to my car and asked her to drive us back to the office. She looked at me totally perplexed and asked, "Why, you don't feel good?" I said, "I feel fine, I just want to see how you drive!"

On the six mile drive to the office she drove like a pro. She was an excellent driver. While we were on our way to the office, I asked her if she would like for me to go skiing with her. Her response, "Would love it!"

YEAR 5:
Patient: Parents inattention.
Observations: Relationship development.

Early in 1964, a systems analyst position became available in my organization and I promoted her into this position. To celebrate her promotion, I invited her to Trader Vics, a restaurant located on 59th Street in NY City. The restaurant had a reputation for excellence, Polynesian cuisine, music, decor and exotic drinks. They certainly were not in a hurry to serve. By the time we had gone through the whole culinary experience, three hours had elapsed. The music was subdued and pleasant. She really enjoyed this restaurant and said that she had to bring her parents to enjoy this experience. She said, "I know they also would enjoy this unique atmosphere." I was perplexed that in spite of her parents lack of attention regarding her physical problems, she was still trying to please them. I told her that Trader Vics was a restaurant chain and were located in many cities. I asked her if she had spent any time out west. I told her about my hunting trips to Arizona and how much I loved the western states. She said she would love to see many of the National Parks out west, like Grand Canyon, Yellowstone, Yosemite and others. As we talked about different subjects, it seemed that no matter what we talked about, we had the same interests. It was really funny.

A strange thought crossed my mind as we were leaving the restaurant. Should our relationship evolve and we would actually get married, I would concentrate on future activities and plan as much traveling as possible before retirement, just in case. I even thought the whole retirement system should be changed. Retire at age 40 and then come back at 65 when you are less inclined to do anything which may raise your blood pressure!

The 1964 company Christmas party was a blast. I danced with several women from the office. I started to drift to the most vivacious person, the woman who had suffered strange symptoms of fatigue and loss of coordination, specifically, my future wife. She must have been in a remission, something she or I had no idea what it was or what it meant at that time. Somehow I was more attracted to her and had a hard time camouflaging my feelings. She was a terrific dancer and wanted to teach me all kinds of new steps, like the Lindy, the Stroll and all the other dances of the era..

YEAR 6:
Patient: Why see Neurologist – feel fine!
Observations: Not optimistic – Neurologist not helpful.

Months later, she and I had to attend a business meeting in Cambridge, Mass. We drove to the meeting because it was actually faster driving from Westchester to their offices and back as compared to going to La Guardia, fly to Boston, rent a car, drive west to Cambridge, return the car and fly back to La Guardia. The late afternoon rush hour out of New York up to our computer center took almost the same amount of time as driving directly from Cambridge to Westchester.

After the meeting, we departed around three thirty on our way back to New York. We had driven for about an hour, when I saw a sign which reminded me of an excellent seafood restaurant in Pittsfield. I asked her if she was interested in a lobster feast. She thought that was a wonderful idea. We headed for Pittsfield and arrived at the restaurant shortly after six. We got a table, ordered our lobster feast and enjoyed our dinner. On the drive home we talked about the business aspects of the meeting, but eventually drifted back to her fatigue the month before. She said she felt fine and I shouldn't worry about it, obviously it isn't serious. She said, "I always get over it and I feel fine." I told her, I wish I could be as optimistic, but something just doesn't make sense. I asked her to make an appointment with another neurologist. She gave me this look, like— why don't you leave me alone? After I insisted, she said, "OK, I WILLLLL!" She just wanted for me to shut up. What a surprise!

After our return from Cambridge, I didn't mention the neurologist again. I didn't want to annoy her. A few weeks later she came into my office, closed the door, sat down and said, "OK, smartass – I did go to the doctor and he said I was nuts and he was going to send me to a nuthouse." I said, "Come on, what did this asylum director really tell you?" Phyllis was disgusted and explained that she had written down all her experiences for the doctor however after a routine examination he said the famous sentence, "It's all in your head!" I was shaking my head in disbelief. I now know that allegedly the diagnostic tools to diagnose MS didn't exist, but what did these neurologists learn in college? How can a variety of symptoms from falling, lack of coordination, tingling on your left arm and fatigue not raise some eyebrows? I was as disgusted as she was, but I wasn't sorry that she had gone to the doctor. Somehow, I thought, we will get to the bottom of this.

YEAR 8:
Patient: Problems disappeared, for good?
Observations: Falling in love with patient.

Two years after the useless visit to the doctor and no recurrence of the symptoms, I bought a special gold ring with diamonds for Phyllis. It was not a wedding band; it was a Florentine finish promise ring with 5 diamonds mounted in a shield like setting with a white gold strip on the side. I went back to my office and called a restaurant in Yorktown Heights, north of New York City, and made dinner reservations at a cozy Italian restaurant. Their food was excellent and I knew from previous conversations with Phyllis that she loved Lasagna and for dessert she couldn't resist ordering a cannoli. The specialty of the house was their lasagna. On Friday nights they had a band and after dinner couples would go there to dance. She loved to dance and she was such a lively woman. I always admired her style and energy. While I was a good dancer, compared to her I was a klutz. She always wanted to teach me new steps and every time I tripped over my feet, she would laugh and laugh until I couldn't stop laughing myself.

The week after I had bought the ring, I invited Phyllis to dinner for that Friday night, the beginning of the Labor Day weekend. She accepted. I had decided to make a bold move. We left the office around five-fifteen and headed for the Yorktown Heights restaurant. We arrived just before six, got a nice table by the dance floor and ordered a glass of wine. We talked about the office, the people in the restaurant, joked around and had a wonderful time. We never ran out of things to talk about. As I had anticipated, Phyllis ordered her favorite dish. After we had completed our main meal, they brought the dessert cart with all those luscious desserts, and guess what, she reached for the cannoli. After she had completed her favorite dessert, I asked her to look at me, because I had something important to tell her. She did and boy was she beautiful. She had a perplexed look on her face when I said, "Phyllis I want to marry you!" True to form, she already was making comments before I could finish my whole pitch, which I had practiced endless times. Her first comment was, "What? From single woman one day, to mother of two kids the next day? What are you talking about?" Now I had a chance to finish my practiced statement and told her of my plans. To further comments from her I said, "Yes I mean it, I am dead serious and give me a chance to prove it to you." I related to her how all this happened and what I wanted to know, if I did everything as promised, would she marry me. She looked at me for a long time, at least it appeared to me as being forever and then she said, "Yes, but." I opened the box with the promise ring and slipped the ring on her right ring finger. She looked at it in total bewilderment but said she absolutely loved the ring. Before she could say anything else, I said, "Look at this ring as my commitment to you, as long as I am true to my commitment, you will not have to take that ring off, except for some medical reasons." Since then, she has never taken that ring off.

Now came all the questions and potential roadblocks. She started rattling off all kinds of issues, like her family, my kids, the co-workers and on and on. It became quite obvious to me, that she had spent some time before this evening thinking about it from her perspective, that's why my direct approach didn't quite overwhelm her; it was like she had been hoping I would have the guts to bring my commitment to fruition. As we started dancing, she then confided that she also had fallen in love, but was fearful that it would never happen. The band played many tunes, but four particular songs stood out, at least to us, they were Memphis, El Watusi, Watermelon Man and Louie, Louie. The following week I bought the 4 records, the 45 rpm version, and that music became our reminder of the most memorable and happiest moments of our lives. This commitment eventually set the stage of a trusting relationship which has been the foundation for her current mindset. As we moved ahead in time, she knew I would never abandon her, no matter what.

YEAR 9:
Patient: Syndromes reappear.
Observations: What is going on – Doctors clueless?

In early 1968, Phyllis and I were on a business trip visiting San Francisco. On the second night after our arrival, I told her I knew of a restaurant that she would love, Trader Vics. Several years back, Phyllis and I had dinner at the New York Trader Vics, a Polynesian restaurant. She loved the food, the Polynesian music and the atmosphere in general.

Other than the great food, the exotic drinks and the subdued music, what became an important highlight of that night was her description of experiences she had. She would get fatigued more than she used to, she still was dropping things or running into doorframes, had tingling down her left arm and was miffed that her parents just shrugged it off as just being clumsy or that she was just imagining things. She had described some of these symptoms before but she seemed more concerned now because she felt the frequency had increased. She described how sometimes when she was driving, she would find herself edging toward the side of the road. She did not recognize the drift until the **car** hit the edge of the road and bounced or she hit a curb and she felt it in the steering wheel. Obviously it had made her very nervous. I didn't feel something like that should be ignored and was somewhat amazed that her parents didn't pay too much attention to this. I was sure that her experiences were very unusual. Something was bothering her and unless she would get some answers, this problem would dominate her life. I advised her that after we return to New York, she should make another appointment with a neurologist. When we left the restaurant, she promised to make a doctor's appointment.

We had decided to add some vacation days to the end of the business trip. We had brought our skis and skiing gear for that occasion. On Wednesday, January 15, after two days of meetings at our facilities, Phyllis and I drove to Squaw Valley for two days of skiing. During those days, it became quite obvious that Phyllis fatigued quite easily. It was definitely more than what I had seen before and could not possibly be considered normal. We took lots of breaks and then started on another round. The weather conditions and the slopes were perfect for skiing, nothing that would make it more tiresome or stressful. Since it was our goal to return to New York from Phoenix, on Saturday morning, we hit the road toward Flagstaff, a 700 mile ride. We left shortly after eight in the morning and arrived in Flagstaff around four in the afternoon. Between Reno and Las Vegas we were driving at speeds between 125 and 135 mph. If they had speed laws, it was quite obvious nobody observed them because occasionally cars even passed us. After we left Las Vegas toward Flagstaff, we had to stay pretty much on posted speed limits and it felt like the car was crawling along at an unbelievably low speed. It's amazing how fast one can get used to high speeds, seeing a blur when you look out through your side windows. Actually it is an exciting experience. As we approached Flagstaff, snow started to fall. It wasn't bad as far as the road conditions were concerned but we were wondering if the Arizona Snowbowl had collected more snow. That area is close to Arizona's highest mountain, the 12,633 foot Humphrey's peak. It is located about 80 miles south of Grand Canyon and just North-North-West of Flagstaff. After we arrived in Flagstaff, we checked the conditions at the Snowbowl and found that they had a significant amount on the ground. We decided that we should visit this ski slope the next day, after all, we wanted to be able to say that we went skiing in Arizona, not exactly known as one of the skiing hot spots in the country. We spent two days at the Snowbowl and on Thursday morning we were on our way toward Phoenix. We drove through the scenic Oak Creek Canyon and a small village at the south end of the canyon called Sedona. At that time, we would never have imagined that it would become one of our most important spots in the US. On Saturday, we returned to New York.

After our return, she made an appointment with a neurologist and scheduled a number of tests at the White Plains hospital. When she received the results, they were mixed. The two doctors who conducted the tests concluded that there were some underlying conditions; they didn't think she was imagining things, but they didn't come up with a conclusive diagnosis. This was very disappointing to her. I told her to begin documenting all the events and then schedule another appointment about a year later.

YEAR 10:
Patient: No problems – cured?
Observations: False sense of security.

Shortly thereafter, we got involved in a major planning job for American Airlines. Phyllis was an active member of the twenty-two employee data processing advanced planning group. The organization consisted of different teams devoted to specific pieces of the overall planning effort. Phyllis was a hardworking, meticulous and dedicated employee. The fatigue she encountered during our "vacation" seemed to have evaporated. Her handwritten notes were very neat, clear and well reasoned. We would meet once a week to review the status of the work performed by each team. This approach made all members feel they were fully involved. They had the opportunity to raise questions and make suggestions or comments regarding the work of all the teams. As a result, the enthusiasm and commitments became very intense. Phyllis' participation was extensive and exemplary. She didn't have any signs whatsoever of her MS.

By late September, all the pieces of the plan were coming together. Now we were faced with the trickiest task, how to put this whole plan together in such a manner that we wouldn't be shot down in flames by the new American Airlines management. The political environment was brutal. The deadline for the completion of the plan was approaching rapidly. In order to avoid any leakage, I dictated the plan to Phyllis and she had a handwritten copy for my final analysis. Obviously my boss wanted to see a final and documented version before it could be submitted to the corporate management.

I decided there was only one way I could get this whole plan put together without interference. I asked Phyllis to take a week off and meet me in San Diego. I flew to San Francisco a day before Phyllis was going to leave. The following day I went to San Diego. After Phyllis arrived, we drove to Borrego Springs. While driving, I had Phyllis take notes of my ideas and thoughts regarding the potential structure of the plan.

One of the notable events of that drive was the fact that Phyllis, who normally couldn't even look at a map or read anything while the vehicle was in motion without getting dizzy, was taking notes and nothing bothered her. Since I do my best thinking while driving, we drove for a total of 2432 miles. During that whole week, Phyllis was taking notes and reading while the vehicle was in motion. She had no dizzy spells or any other reaction. She was in remission, but as far as we were concerned, we thought she had finally overcome whatever had bothered her before. In retrospect, now knowing what her ailment truly was, it only demonstrated that we are all conditioned to never accept the inevitable direction of a serious disease and how a remission, such as those encountered by MS afflicted people, can give you a false sense of security.

YEAR 11:
Patient: Potential serious accident.
Observations: Accident prevented. Caregiver marries patient.

During the summer of 1970, American Airlines decided to move us to Tulsa, Oklahoma. The change was quite involved. Phyllis had traveled extensively, a major benefit of working for an airline, but now she was moving away from her roots and her family. She was quite positive about this and handled it very well. It was then that we decided the time was right to get married. The MS reminder came back when we got off the plane in Tulsa. Her left knee collapsed just when she wanted to step down on the first step of the portable staircase, which had been pushed against the fuselage of the plane's exit door. One of the stewardesses was standing to her right and I was to her left. Our instant reaction, to suddenly grab her, prevented her from taking a potentially bad stumble down the ramp.

After this episode, she managed to coast along in fairly good shape and pretty much forgot that whole episode. As a matter of fact, she started to teach me the art of archery. We had set up a target on our property and she was an expert with those arrows. I am sure the Oklahoma Indians would have accepted her as one of their own. As I said earlier, while we were in New York, I was amazed at her ability to fish with a bow and arrow. She had the strength and dexterity to handle the bow while at the same time hit the target. After some of the lessons, I had the strength but the other two ingredients for successful archery were missing. I mention this because over a period of ten years following this endeavor, the strength, dexterity, and precision completely disappeared and she had lost the capability to pull the string of the bow.

YEAR 12:
Patient: Another accident!
Observations: Frustrated with medical profession.

In early 1971, after we moved into our new home, my wife had another one of her "its all in your head" experiences. When she drove the car into our garage, she bumped the tires real hard into the concrete stopper, which was installed on the garage floor so that the vehicle couldn't drive from the garage into our red, white and blue bathroom located behind the wall of the garage. She hit her head against the steering wheel.

To me it was becoming quite clear that there had to be a flaw in the "it's in your head" diagnosis. Knees suddenly buckling, exhaustion seemingly unrelated to anything she was doing, tingling in her arms, occasional double vision, walking into door frames; this couldn't possibly be imaginary. I questioned her about all these issues or experiences. I got her usual response, "You are a pain in the ass, you worry too much, I feel fine!"

She was a very strong willed person and wasn't going to be stopped by "these small inconveniences." I looked at it more from a long range perspective and having observed her now for more than ten years the frequency and severity of the signs had increased and my mathematical mind projected an exponential problem. The fact that the doctors couldn't come up with a potential diagnosis was even more worrisome, obviously it had to be something rarer than a common cold. In light of it, I viewed our relationship in a somewhat different context. Sometimes when she would get frustrated or upset and vented her feelings to the only one in the room, ME, rather than getting upset, I expressed my understanding, deep love and commitment to her. It calmed her down and within minutes she felt better and she would smile. (The beginning of Caregiving)

YEAR 13:
Patient: No longer employed.
Observations: Increased attention – mindset boosters.

After she quit her job at American Airlines, I told her, I really don't want for you to find a job other than some volunteer type chores. I said, "This way we can continue to travel and do those things we loved to do before we got married. If you would have a job, it would create restraints such as not having enough vacation days or personal time to do it." She thought that was great. Retaining a positive attitude had to be fed with exciting and pleasurable events. It would become very important to keep stressful events to a bare minimum. Based on my observations up to that point, I had reached the conclusion that major distractions, like enjoyable events, would extend remissions. Obviously the concept of a remission only became meaningful after her MS had been diagnosed. When I surprised her with something she enjoyed, like a dress, a dinner at a restaurant she had mentioned to me or an antique she had discovered (I hated antiques), her whole demeanor was of extreme joy.

Most couples after they get married quite frequently pursued careers for a number of reasons, such as improving their financial situation in anticipation of the children they want to have and the resources required to eventually give them a head start in life. Those are noble endeavors, but I thought, there is one important issue called retirement. Everyone is aware of it, but it is so many years down-line that it can be put off until later. Somehow the expression, "When we retire we will do this or that" is thought of in terms of the current health status, which in general terms is usually much better in your earlier years. Normal deterioration is so slow, that it doesn't prompt you to re-evaluate your retirement dreams and eventually lead to the statement, "If I would have known then what I know now, I would have done this or that while I was able to do it." My wife's experience, while taken lightly by her, was a warning sign for me and I read it as such. I was going to make sure we would continue our secret "escapades" in spite of now being legitimate. I wanted to come up with exciting moments. When we went on trips or embarked on some unusual adventures, Phyllis was so happy. She was such a vivacious person and I loved her and her beautiful smile. Over time, instead of drifting apart, we got closer and closer. We truly were able to read each others mind. It was very heart-warming and it made our love affair eternal. Many may read this as, "You are just one lucky couple," while that is definitely true, we consciously created that environment, something that became the most important part of the "Caregiver" part. You truly must love and CARE to GIVE!

Since we were now located almost in the middle of the country, escapades to the western USA was much easier. It was this part of the country we loved the most.

Phyllis had been quite busy setting up and decorating the house. To her it meant frequent trips to every store in sight. She was in high heaven and I was trying to figure out how to keep up with the credit cards. When I tried to talk to her about this, she laughed and said, "I am doing what I am good at, you are the financial wizard, I am sure you can figure out how to pay for it, you always managed before." In spite of her comment, she would come back and ask, "How much can I spend?" Now I had to laugh and said, "Look Phyllis, I re-did the budget and now we are good for another six months." She said, "You know, I have no idea how you do it, but each time we are in a pickle, you re-do the budget and voila, everything is solved." I told her, "Guess what, I squeezed some extra money out in order to celebrate your fabulous work, I have made hotel and car rental reservations for our trip this weekend." She wanted to know, "What trip?" I said, "Just pack the stuff we need for the weekend so we can leave in the late afternoon this coming Friday – surprise – surprise."

On Friday I came home after lunch and she was all ready. We went to the airport for our flight to Dallas. I finally told her that we were going to San Francisco and from there would drive to Yosemite National Park. She always wanted to visit the park but somehow we never managed to work it into our previous escapades. She was delighted. We arrived in San Francisco in the early evening hours. I had made reservations at the airport hotel. It took us about four and half hours from the hotel to Yosemite. We arrived just in time to have lunch at a log cabin type structure, a steak house located next to the Merced River. It was cozy and beautiful. We ordered steaks, of course!

After lunch we took a hike and walked toward the upper and lower Yosemite Falls. We took in all the sights, drove around the park, climbed around and took loads of pictures. At no time during this whole visit did she show any signs of fatigue, nothing bothered her.

By now it was late afternoon and we decided to take the scenic route, a road partially along the river and bordered by giant sequoias. We stayed at a Fresno hotel and in the morning we were off to San Francisco We took an early afternoon flight through Dallas back to Tulsa. We arrived in the early evening bringing to an end another wonderful experience. It always appeared that after such an adventure, Phyllis seemed to improve. Whenever we went on some of these fun trips her MS symptoms appeared to be forced into remission. I was sure, if we expressed that belief to any one of the neurologists, we would hear the expression, "It's all in your head." No matter what, I saw some favorable results and was going to keep it going.

As a result of a job change, in April 1972, we decided to move back to New York. Not long after our becoming New Yorkers again, MS reappeared in a somewhat comical fashion. While I was attending one of the many useless meetings at my downtown office, a secretary came in and handed me a note, it said, "Your wife is on the phone, said it is important."

It had to be important, Phyllis usually didn't call me. She always waited for my calls. Nevertheless, I was happy to be out of the meeting.

When I picked up the phone, Phyllis told me that she had a car accident. I asked her if she was OK. She said, "I am fine, I don't have a problem." I responded, "What a relief, how about the driver of the other car and what happened to our car?" She said, "Well, there is no other driver, but both of our cars have some damage. I ran one car into the other." I was silent for a minute, I had to swallow and I was at the desk of the secretary on the executive floor. I had to swallow again to make sure I wouldn't say, "What?" with a raised voice, so a milder, "How did that happen?" came out of my mouth. Phyllis explained that she really didn't know how it happened, she just lost control. Again a reminder, this was 8 years before her Multiple Sclerosis was diagnosed. In spite of this weird accident, it didn't prompt us to seek any medical advice since she had gone to the doctors so many times before and was told repeatedly, "It's all in your head." We felt it was senseless to be told the same thing again and again. We decided to ignore this episode. The irony is that when her disease was finally diagnosed, the expression "it's all in your head" is literally true, but for a different reason. After MRI scans were introduced and became available, MS could finally be seen as white scarring on the brain.

YEAR 15:
Patient: Overconfident-last attempt at skiing.
Observations: Roller coaster ride continues.

Phyllis had seen a commercial on TV about cross country skiing so she came up with another one of her impulsive ideas. Right after Halloween while having dinner she said, "Wouldn't you like to try cross country skiing?" The two boys didn't mind, they had never been on cross country skis. As a matter of fact, I was the only one who had learned the art early in my life in Germany. I immediately volunteered to show them all the tricks of the trade, which pretty much consisted of sticking your boots into the bindings. As far as I was concerned, that was the true skiing, not the down-hill rushes.

On Saturday morning we packed all our gear, clothing and skis into our truck and took off toward the Mt. Snow Ski Resort in Vermont. We arrived about 11:30 AM. There was a very light snowfall and it was pretty cold. We had lunch, we put our skis on and went on one of the cross country trails. The wind had picked up somewhat and it felt much colder. We were sliding along, but for no apparent reason, Phyllis would suddenly fall to one side. It happened so many times, that I decided to basically ski next to her with my arm around her until we got back to the truck. Phyllis attributed the falling to the wind, but the wind wasn't that severe to push her over. I asked her how she felt. She said, "Maybe I was over confident, I thought I was stronger, but I feel very weak." Was it another one of her unknown MS attacks? We roamed around for several hours and then decided to get ready for our trip back.

YEAR 16:
Patient: Giving birth – increase in syndromes.
Observations: Bottom of the class doctors?

In early 1975, our daughter was born. Within months the frequency of her unusual fatigue increased exponentially. It became more difficult for her to walk up and down the stairs in our house. Getting up the hill to the street level was quite strenuous.

She would have tingling in her arms and sometimes she complained about loss of hearing in her left ear. But whenever we went to the doctor, it didn't even trigger a response of "Maybe you have this or that, nothing!" Later on when her Multiple Sclerosis was finally diagnosed, it was clear that all these signs had just been ignored and didn't prompt any one of the doctors to think twice about the fact that this could not possibly be normal.

YEAR 19:
Patient: Slower reaction time – driving impacted.
Observations: Answer – Off-Road Vehicle (Jeep).
There is no question that Phyllis' problems had an impact on her driving. I completely missed the warning signs when she crashed one of our vehicles into the other. In retrospect it is hard to comprehend how I missed such an important event. Obviously she would never have been able to judge her own driving habits or style. One only views OTHERS as bad and incompetent drivers. It is rare to find a driver who agrees with a police officer when he or she is ticketed for a violation that hasn't been committed, right? Tests later revealed that her reaction time was lengthened considerably due to her MS. To solve the problem, as always, Phyllis had the solution. Since she spent so much time "off the road," we needed an "off-road vehicle." Why didn't I come up with such a wonderful idea? We bought a beautiful orange colored CJ-7 Jeep Renegade. Phyllis loved that car.

YEAR 20:
Patient: Daughter's accident-more problems.
Observations: Adrenaline rush.

In the middle of 1979, I received a panic call from Phyllis telling me that our daughter had an accident and that she was on her way to the emergency room. She couldn't talk, just come as fast as possible. I was at the Long Island data center and left immediately.

I was worried stiff, especially since Phyllis didn't have the time to talk. I drove like a nut and went straight to the Dobbs Ferry hospital emergency room, where both of them were waiting for a bone specialist.

Our daughter had tripped and fell down a flight of stairs. She had broken her left arm. When the accident occurred, Phyllis was having increasing problems walking up and down the steps. She had to hold on so she wouldn't stumble and fall. She could hardly lift a pot of water. When our daughter fell, she ran down the stairs, lifted and carried her to the upper front deck, called our next door neighbor, who responded immediately. Phyllis told her that she needed a ride to the hospital. Our neighbor pulled her car out from her driveway, parked in front of our house and helped Phyllis who was holding Kerri. The hospital was only about a six minute drive from our house. At the hospital she lifted her out and carried her into the waiting room. The love for her daughter and obvious concern was like a stimulus shot. She overcame some of the MS induced problems, but when I arrived she was so weak I had to assist her because she could hardly walk. After this experience we had to get a cane. It had to be a decorative cane with a brass dog head so it looked like a fad, not a necessity. After our daughter had been released from the hospital, my wife was complaining about her weakness and that she was having difficulties attending to my daughter's requirements. Fortunately, Phyllis' mother, who only lived about 5 minutes from our home, helped her extensively.

YEAR 21:
Patient: Finally DIAGNOSIS-In denial.
Observations: Top of the class doctor!

At this point, even Phyllis realized that this could not go on and on without having an idea what the problem was. She made an appointment with her regular doctor and for the first time, the physician expressed the feeling that she may have MS. She suggested that she see a MS specialist, Dr. Labe Scheimberg, at the Albert Einstein Medical College in the Bronx, one of the top specialists in this field. She called his office, explained the situation and made the appointment. When she walked into his office, he demonstrated his expertise and knowledge with his first comment, he said, "You have MS." He said further, in order to be absolutely sure, we will conduct some tests and for those you will have to be hospitalized for a few days. We told him that she had undergone a series of tests at the Westchester Hospital in White Plains in 1969 for the same reason. He said "Great. I am on their medical board; I will request the data and look at it." Arrangements were made to have her being admitted to the hospital. During her three (3) day stay they did a number of tests, but the spinal tap was what must have done her in. Something must have gone wrong, because Phyllis was in excruciating pain after the spinal tap and her condition never reversed itself to pre-hospital entry.

The end result was that there was no question, she had Multiple Sclerosis and the Doctors who had done the tests in 1969 apparently had not been sufficiently astute and experienced to detect it then. When

Phyllis returned home, her mother attended to her needs, because she could hardly move due to her spinal tap induced pain. It took weeks before she was able to walk again and then she relied on a cane to help her. Being the eternal optimist, Phyllis was in complete denial. As she managed to improve from the severe pain and immobility as a result of the spinal tap, she interpreted it as "a major improvement." Since the doctor had told her that a recovery or improvement was not in the cards once you contract or have MS, she was certain that she would beat the odds.

YEAR 22:
Patient: Needs a cane.
Observations: Increased attention and affection.

With sheer will power she managed to walk and drive again. When anybody was watching, she would take the cane for a walk and not let on that she actually was relying on it to make sure she could support herself. I gave her all the attention in the world, but because of her reaction, I had to back off from time to time because she started to behave exactly like MS people. When I assisted her, she would turn to me and say, "I don't know why you think I need help," and then at other moments she would say, "Don't you see I need help?" Seeing this highly independent person undergoing this mental struggle just made me love her even more. While many couples faced with this type of a disease somehow drift apart, our love for each other just became more intense.

After a few months, she had somewhat recovered and became a little bit more self confident. I had to attend a Diebold Research meeting at Kiawah Island and I figured this would be a great opportunity to take my wife and daughter along in order to boost her self confidence even further. While I was working hard, they could enjoy the beach. I asked Phyllis to talk to the teacher and get some homework for our daughter. On the Island, the Diebold Research Group had made reservations for all its members at the Kiawah Island Inn, Charleston S.C. We had a two bedroom, two story condo. Our daughter loved these arrangements. Once she was upstairs, she could look out from the balcony and throw items down. Fortunately, she picked soft toys and not the steam iron. While I attended to business (a little bit), they went to the beach and their favorite excursions to the gift shop. When I was not attending meetings and seminars, we drove around to visit stores and tried many of their excellent restaurants. This "intense working session," ended on Friday morning, so we took advantage and enjoyed a weekend shopping tour before returning home. After all, Phyllis was the professional shopper and NEEDED all kinds of Christmas gifts for her extensive family. I have never been able to figure out how she always was able to find the most unique and expensive items without looking at a price tag. It was like the products had a homing beacon installed. One thing was for sure, it pushed MS off her mind, so from that perspective, I was very happy for her.

YEAR 24:
Patient: Must move-Handicap friendly home.
Observations: Must retire early.

Now that we were back at our three story house in New York, it became abundantly clear that Phyllis would eventually be confined to a big power wheelchair. Retirement had to be viewed from that perspective. While still working for the bank, I had to attend frequent meetings in Sarasota, Florida. Each time I came, I brought my two beauties with me. Phyllis started to like Sarasota. So we bought land and then designed the house we anticipated would eventually be required to meet the severe disability she would face in the future. All doors were made 36 inches wide, we made sure that we would have no steps, just ramps, and many handle bars. The rails of the sliders to the pool area were recessed into the floor. Many electronic features were installed, allowing a disabled person in a bed or in a wheelchair, to monitor all the activities in the house through cameras, sensors and a security system which announced everything from an open door or window to the opening and closing of the garage door. The house was equipped with an emergency generator to provide limited power for important and necessary electrical components. We also had a back-up air conditioning unit just for the bedroom in case of a power failure. MS patients are very sensitive to temperature variations and stable humidity should be maintained as much as possible. As Phyllis' MS progressed, restricting her even further, other features were added such as an extensive entertainment system for the bedroom, voice or computer activated phone and a talking computer, since her lung capacity diminished. Occasionally she was unable to push sufficient air through her voice cords to create the words necessary to communicate or express her problems. We also ended up with an assortment of big button remotes capable of turning anything on and off in the house. The reaction to all this by many readers will be, "Sure, if you have lots of money you can do all these things!" We didn't have lots of money! Early on in life I learned to be quite disciplined when it came to money management and always was and still am a meticulous long range planner. Since inflation is ever present, one must build future scenarios and price them out. This will allow you to analyze the return on your investment in today's dollars. This type of a calculation will identify those things that are less costly to do now rather than wait for "when we have the money." Most of these features can be incorporated into the mortgage, so the ongoing cost is kept in check. Some people feel they must go out to a restaurant at least once a week. The return on that investment is pretty much zero, except for the satisfaction that you probably had a wonderful meal and a good time. Best of all, you didn't have to wash dishes and maybe impressed your neighbor. These are choices that one has to make. There are sacrifices to be made, no question. A high degree of independence will be your reward, if you drop some of the ==★ niceties. It also will cause you to be less "surprised" when certain services which you may believe are an entitlement, do not materialize. We ate out very frequently but decided to abandon these conveniences and spend more time in the kitchen and cook ourselves. If you don't know how, start a new hobby. Learning how to cook carries higher financial rewards as compared to many of the jobs you may find in the help-wanted section of your newspaper. It will also make you pay more attention to the nutrition labels and hopefully keep all those strange chemical components like "potassium chloride" and my favorite "natural flavors" out of your body. There are many ways to cut expenses if you know why and what you are spending.

YEAR 25:
Patient: NO INSURANCE for MS.
Observations: More intervention and help.

When I departed from my position at the bank, my insurance continued for a period of 18 months. Little did we know that Phyllis would never be able to get health insurance because of her Multiple Sclerosis? It is outright discriminatory! You may think, well the premium would be high. NO! It doesn't matter if you are able to pay a high premium. The insurance companies look at human beings having the slightest potential problem as rusty machines that may need some repair work done in the future. That thought sends spine tingling shivers down their back. GOD forbid there is a remote chance that profits could be impacted by just one policy holder. The name Multiple Sclerosis (MS) is stricken from the Insurance company lexicon. Once an agent hears those two letters "MS," he turns around and leaves. Not much has happened from **YEAR 25** to the **YEAR 49** to improve our situation as is evident with all the misinformation and outright lies which are being spread by opponents of **true** health care reform in 2009 (The year 2009 is one year after **YEAR 49** in our chronological evolutionary description). Patients and Caregivers are hopefully much more aware of the general conditions which impact them as a result of their disabilities, in spite of new laws which really never protect them from some of the predatory corporate practices.

In spite of some of these setbacks, we didn't look back but moved forward. The last two years before retiring early, I decided to accept the presidency of a computer services corporation. This required extensive travel. We now started home schooling our daughter and to make it easier on all of us, we rented apartments in three cities where key clients were located. While that diminished the travel requirements for us and kept me close to Phyllis and our daughter, it created a strange problem. We could never remember in what closet and what town specific garments where located. One of the apartments was in Denver and of all the locations this was the one where Phyllis seemed to feel most energetic. Was it the altitude or being close to the Coors beer brewery? The first year she seemed to be in remission. She remained stable. She was able to frequently walk with the walker and when she had to use the wheelchair, she had sufficient strength to move it herself. At that time she was still using the regular manual wheelchair with the big wheels. The following year, she had frequent fatigue problems and the constant travel back and forth between five locations, Austin, Dallas, Denver, New York and Sarasota, had a deteriorating impact. I knew that the time had come that the Caregiver role required a higher percentage of my time vs the time dedicated to my corporate responsibilities.

In early 1986 we decided it was time to kiss the hectic life style good bye, retire and begin the cancellation process of our leases, pack up and consolidate everything into our house in Sarasota. Phyllis, who always had been a meticulous organizer and planner, did it one more time, the last time! She developed a detailed plan to make all the moves in the most efficient manner, no needless second trips or backtracking. She documented everything and her handwriting was still beautiful. The transition from Corporate Big-Wig to Caregiver went like clockwork.

YEAR 27:
Patient: Apply for disability.
Observations: Success!

After we had settled into our new handicap friendly house, we decided a reward for our efforts was called for, so we planned a ten day vacation trip to Maui, Hawaii. While Phyllis was exited about the whole idea, this was the first trip that she was totally confined to the wheelchair. In spite of it, she always tried to walk, but after a few steps, she had to sit down in the wheelchair. The walker had become a liability because her knees would buckle and she would collapse.

The difference from 1984 to the middle of 1986 was significant. The disability had taken a deeper slide downward since the preceding two years. After our return from our vacation, I started to dedicate myself to finally obtaining Phyllis' Social Security disability. She had reached a point now, where she was pretty much wheelchair bound. She still tried to struggle as much as she could, but she tired much more frequently.

Having investigated the whole process before, I already knew all the roadblocks I would encounter. Now I was prepared to dedicate time to this endeavor and maneuver through the bureaucratic nightmare, no matter "how good Phyllis looked." This statement was made by an attorney in 1980 when we contacted him in order to help us maneuver through the application process for disability. His analysis was that Phyllis would be turned down because "she looked to good." I asked the attorney, "What the hell does that mean, how does one have to look to qualify for disability? Do you need a steel plate screwed to your head and all the teeth missing?" In spite of a ridiculous statement such as this, we thought, it would be extremely difficult for us to pursue this issue. We just didn't have the time to deal with it and in all probability he was right. After being turned down during the second step, the reconsideration phase, we just dropped the issue.

Now I had more time and I wasn't about to give up. When Social Security denied her initial application and then her appeal, there only was one choice, take the case to federal court. By the way, Social Security relied on the information my wife's doctor had provided to them in spite of the fact that the doctor had passed away three years before the interview took place. They insisted that they had interviewed the dead doctor! Have you ever wondered what powers our government has? This is living proof that they can interview the dead. If you ever need to find out where your great-grandmother hid all her treasures, just contact Social Security, they will get a hold of her.

I contacted an attorney and asked him if he could handle this case for Phyllis. He wasn't terribly excited about it. I pleaded with him to support me by allowing me to do all the legal research and footwork.

Then, based on my work, he could make the case for Phyllis in court. He agreed, because he probably figured, he had nothing to lose, if I am so confident that I can accomplish this, why not. Easy money! I proceeded with the research and the development of the case. When the day came to be seen by the administrative judge, I thought I had a damned good case. He asked the attorney and Phyllis into the courtroom and then he looked at this old muscle man who was pushing Phyllis' wheelchair. Somehow in the judge's eyes my legal standing was apparently not of the quality as viewed from my confidence level, so he asked me to wait outside his courtroom. Talk about seeing your ego being deflated instantly, it was in a nosedive. Fortunately only 3 minutes had elapsed when he called me in, because he had great difficulties understanding Phyllis and the attorney advised him that only the "wheelchair pusher you sent out, the Caregiver, is the only one who understands his wife."

The upshot was, we won the case. This was a major victory for us, since from now on, Phyllis was covered by Medicare. She had been without insurance after the "COBRA" period of 18 months had expired. I retired early in order to dedicate myself 100% to the Caregiver job. This was six years after her final diagnosis.

YEAR 28:
Patient: Motorized scooter.
Observations: 100% dedication-relationship stronger.

The time had arrived that even the manual wheelchair started to become difficult for Phyllis to push by herself, so now her first motorized scooter arrived. She loved it because she now was able to drive around the property and accompany me on my weight reducing walks. We still would go on long drives. Early in the summer months we embarked on a northern cross-country trip as part of our home schooling effort to visit national parks and monuments. All trips were planned with the input from the three of us. This was very important. Whatever we decided to do had to be agreed to by unanimous consent. I had bought a portable wheelchair which I could fold up and keep in the trunk of our car. We also bought a portable electrical refrigerator to keep her medication, travel food, juice and soda. When we had to stop for gas, I would lift Phyllis in and out of the car so that she could attend to her bodily functions. She was relatively comfortable while driving. She had a special lap table and prepared the sandwiches while traveling, thus allowing us to progress much faster. These trips brought all of us closer and closer together, further strengthening the foundation of our relationship so crucial for the ongoing patient/Caregiver combination.

YEAR 29:
Patient: Fulfilling dream.
Observations: Motor home not beneficial.

In the fall of this year we undertook an extensive cross-country trip with the intent of visiting the National Parks and Monuments in the southwestern United States. We always tried new ways. For this trip we rented a big motor home. We wanted to test this concept to see if Phyllis would be more comfortable. We used the portable wheelchair inside the motor home and the power scooter, which was carried in a storage bin under the motor home, for outside mobility. She had to be physically carried down the steps and be placed in her power scooter. While this trip was entertaining and mentally very rewarding for Phyllis, it also fulfilled one of Phyllis' desires to have our daughter visit as many States in the

Union as possible. Her wish was all 50 states but in the end we had to be satisfied with 47. Alaska, North Dakota and Oregon never had the pleasure to play host to Phyllis and our daughter.

After analyzing all the pros and cons of this mode of travel, we determined it to be less desirable for a person with her disabilities. It was great for the Caregiver but more physically stressful to the patient.

YEAR 31:
Patient: High degree of spasticity.
Observations: New power wheelchair required.

As we progressed in time, her disability created more and more complicating situations. While she was able to move the power scooter throughout the house, her aim was off. The scooter required her to press a lever to propel it forward, but the spasticity affected her ability to slow it down, stop or turn in time. She now ran into furniture, walls and doorframes with a contraption which was immune to pain, just caused it. Since we had bought the original scooter outright without going through insurance or any input from a therapist, her neurologist referred her to a therapist for an analysis in order to find a power wheelchair more suitable to her requirements. This one was partially financed through the Medicare program. In spite of the fact that she was covered by Medicare, she still could not get supplemental insurance. Disabled people, when covered by Social Security Disability as a result of their condition, still cannot apply for supplemental health insurance because that is only available to retired Social Security recipients when they reach their retirement age. Those that really need the help don't get it. Are you surprised?

YEAR 32:
Patient: Country demeaning to the disabled.
Observations: Saudi Arabian adventure?

The Gulf War had just ended when I received a call from the top bank executive of Arab National Bank in Riyadh, Saudi Arabia. After introducing himself, he didn't waste any time and asked me to accept an executive position at his bank. I was taken back but politely responded that I will have to call him back the following day in order to discuss this with my wife. Phyllis' reaction was, "You must be kidding!" Well, we decided that it probably wasn't smart to turn it down cold turkey, but to potentially accept the position with a clear understanding that my wife's medical condition, plus other requirements, must be met. We developed a list of conditions which would choke a mule. We were having fun developing it because we were so certain that they would hang up on us after we had read 25% of our conditions. We were fairly certain that they probably would send us a thermometer to take our temperature and politely decline. The following day I called them back and talked to the top executive. I read our list of 20 items and the anticipated "hang-up click" never came. After listening to all the conditions, I was giving a fax number and requested to send my conditions and requirements over so that they could prepare the contract for my signature. When I turned to Phyllis I didn't have to ask her to sit down, she was already seated and I unleashed the news. I got a loud, "What?" in return.

How money can drastically improve a severe disability is an eye-opener. Part of the deal was to provide a female assistant for my wife, a huge private home and our own limo, with a driver who was living on the premises and available 24/7. Phyllis and our daughter always traveled with me on all business trips and all was first class, flights and hotels. The bank paid to have assistants available wherever we had to go. The few times we had to go to the hospital, we found the service and the competence of staff, from doctors to nurses, superior to anything we had experienced in our own country. The most impressive part was their superior technology. I saw equipment, manufactured in the US and Germany, that I had never seen in the US. During this whole time, Phyllis' condition remained stable, there was no deterioration and I believe the extra pampering had a favorable impact. A top notch health care system will make a difference. Unfortunately, what was lacking outside the hospital was the infrastructure, like the availability of ramps and wide elevators to support disabled people in their wheelchairs. It was further complicated by the fact that women and man could not ride together in an elevator. Acceptance by the population at large of severely disabled people in public view didn't exist. When Zewdi, her female assistant was pushing my wife's wheelchair, it appeared to create a large empty space around us, more than was necessary to move freely. I couldn't help but get the impression that the Saudis would prefer to have them kept at home. Since they definitely had some kind of a cast system, maybe disabled people were in such a cast. When I discussed it with some of my Saudi employees, they assured me that I had formed the wrong impression. Somehow it was difficult for me to reconcile what I saw and what was said.

This experience warrants a political comment: We are sold on the idea that among many other questionable reasons, we must be in Afghanistan to free women from the abuse of the Taliban. Women in Saudi Arabia are facing the same abuse. **Difference**: In Saudi Arabia we can tolerate it, after all they have **OIL**. Afghanistan doesn't have such a favored status with their large crop of **DRUGS**.

YEAR 33:
Patient: Now goes the bladder.
Observations: New Caregiving environment.

After our return from Saudi Arabia and during the summer, her bladder gave out and she now needed a catheter. How one little tube can have a life changing impact is hard to understand. A whole new aspect of her disease evolved. Now we had to monitor her bladder and the fluids. She had frequent bladder infections which required antibiotics to bring it under control. It appeared to affect her in other ways. Suddenly it became more difficult for her to write. Her spasticity was so severe that even with medication it was only partially controllable. Fortunately, the power wheelchair had an adjustment which compensated to a degree for the spasticity, basically allowing her to maneuver the wheelchair safely. This period was a roller coaster ride. It resulted in many doctor appointments, "try this or that" suggestions and even different medications until all the adjustments had been made to stabilize her somewhat. As a Caregiver, I was still relying on the physicians for their learned knowledge. I just made the assumption they all knew what they were doing. Unfortunately that is not correct. We were lucky and the key physicians were top notch. Later experiences prompted me to change my style and attitude.

YEAR 34:
Patient: Roll reversal-consoling Caregiver.
Observations: Emotionally difficult period.

This year my son, who had been diagnosed with child diabetes at age 7, passed away after his 9th heart attack. His desire was to be buried in Sedona, Arizona. This is the town we visited in **YEAR 8** not knowing then how important it would become to us in later years. It should be no secret that this was a very difficult period for me, the Caregiver. Phyllis' strong emotional support helped me to get through a very trying period. From this year forward, we embarked on annual cross-country trips to visit my son's grave. The trips were carefully planned. We took into account the fact that Phyllis' catheter had to be changed once a month, therefore these trips had to be completed within a four week span. The fact that she had a catheter made it a little bit easier for me because I didn't have to lift her out of the car each time we stopped for gas. We still used the portable wheelchair and the in and out exercise was limited to the morning before starting the trip and after we arrived at our nightly destination. We carried four medical supply bags in the trunk of our car containing all the supplies we could possibly need. Over time we had developed a long checklist of all the items that should be packed, or be available, in case of an emergency. Each year we updated and modified the lists according to changing conditions. As a result of this meticulous planning, we never ran into an unforeseen situation. A small town hospital emergency room would have been happy to get a hold of that trunk full of stuff. She enjoyed these trips enormously. She enjoyed the scenery and it appeared that MS problems totally receded while on these trips. It almost seemed that her remissions were significantly influenced by her mindset. What was puzzling is the fact that for quite a while she didn't talk about any MS problems. It was like she didn't want to burden me while I was recovering from my grief.

YEAR 39:
Patient: Dentist experience.
Observations: On guard! Protect patient from scams.

Over the last five years there was a steady but slow downhill slide. The major deterioration was with her hands. She almost lost total control.

She was able to move her hands but grabbing anything became much more difficult. During our cross-country trips she was no longer capable of preparing sandwiches or opening boxes. She encountered sporadic hearing loss in her left ear. She also would complain about sudden severe toothaches on her left side. Her face was even swollen. We would make immediate dental appointments, but by the time she was sitting in the dentist office waiting room, the swelling started to subside and the pain had diminished. Now something new started. The dentist took x-rays and then recommended a treatment plan amounting to thousands of dollars. Somehow I wasn't quite convinced. His description of what had to be done just didn't sound logical therefore, instead of making a commitment I made an appointment with another dentist. The second dentist took x-rays and this time I got the surprise of my life. He said, "Her condition is created by her MS. She has absolutely no problem with her teeth or gums. She seems to suffer from a nerve pain on the left side of her face and I recommend a specially formulated cream." We applied the cream and her pain totally disappeared. Since then I have had several opportunities to talk to other MS patients who told me they had sudden dental problems and underwent all kinds of dental work. My suggestion, get a second or third opinion. MS may create a condition which is then misinterpreted or used fraudulently to perform unnecessary work. BE CAREFUL!

YEAR 40:
Patient: Emergency Room.
Observations: Beware of do-gooders!

Phyllis had problems lifting herself up from the wheelchair and moving herself to the toilet. We had handle bars wherever she needed to hold on. This time she was able to lift herself up but her knees collapsed and she didn't have the strength to hold herself. She fell and hit her head on the floor. She had a cut and was bleeding, scary scene. I lifted her up, placed her back onto the wheelchair and took her to the emergency room. After going through a few tests, which showed no damage other than a small cut, Phyllis and I had to endure an interview by a social worker. Her questions and demeanor were directed toward getting me, the caregiver, to confess to whatever abusive scenario she had conjured up in her mind. When the social worker finally realized that this was an accident and nothing more, they released us. Unfortunately many disabled people are abused and the social workers provide a very necessary service, however they should be properly trained in their tactics and approach. In spite of our visit to the emergency room and their tests, I made an appointment with her Neurologist. He recommended an MRI just to make sure that she had not suffered some hidden damage. The result was, the fall had caused no damage but showed that her MS had progressed significantly as compared to an earlier reading.

YEAR 41:
Patient: Nerve pain and catheter problems.
Observations: Major decision-potentially life prolonging.

Phyllis now started to complain about frequent occurrences of pain in her left leg, a leg that has no feeling. Over and over again, she complained about problems on her left side, rarely about any pain on her right side. It is her left hand that has contracted three of her five fingers, she loses her hearing on the left side, she has nerve pain on the left side of her face and now she is reporting pain in her left leg. What is it about the left side?

In addition she was having more and more problems with her catheter. The Urologist told us originally that within 5 to 8 years she would need an operation because prolonged use of a catheter through the urethra would cause more and more infections. After they had placed the first catheter, they recommended that she should drink cranberry juice, allegedly it was healthy. When I brought her in for catheter changes and she had an infection they asked what was obvious to them, "Are you giving her cranberry juice?" I had but now the rebel in me came to the conclusion, that it may not be the right drink for her. I told the Urologist that I was going to switch to orange juice, despite his strong opposition. He said orange juice was to acidic. I figured the only way to find out is to test it. After we changed her from cranberry juice to orange juice, her infections diminished. In **YEAR 46**, another Urologist determined that she didn't have enough acid and prescribed daily medication to further increase the acid past what the orange juice provided. It is ironic that the observations by the Caregiver found the acid requirements 6 years earlier. Since we were now in the 8th year of her monthly catheter changes, the issue of the operation came up again. The Urologist felt it was in Phyllis' best interest to have the bladder either eliminated or bypassed and have the catheter inserted into her belly because it would eliminate bladder infections. The best way to describe what happened is to transcribe the recorded conversation which took place between the Urologist and the Caregiver.

Question: What infection?

Answer: She will have more infections.

Question: Can't we deal with them as they occur?

Answer: Yes, but she will begin to get tolerant to the medication.

Question: After a successful operation, the bladder or urinary tract infections will disappear? Answer: Well, no. There is still a chance that she may get an infection from time to time.

Question: So what is the benefit? I am lost!

Answer: OK, if you don't think she should have the operation, obviously you can make that decision. We will just monitor her progress.

My response: Well, I thought that is what we are doing today!

After this visit, I took her to the Neurologist to deal with the nerve pain problem. The Neurologist prescribed Neurontin. When I asked him what this medication is supposed to do, he gave a very honest but perplexing answer. Sometimes it helps. In general, we really don't know what it does to MS patients, they react differently, just observe her. The dosage was gradually built up to 9 pills a day of 300mg each.

The above two issues are important. Later on I will come back to them because of decisions we made based on careful observations.

YEAR 42:
Patient: Nerve pain and Neurontin.
Observations: Decisions, decisions!

We had now administered Neurontin for over 9 months. At one of our appointments with the Neurologist, I pointed out that I hadn't noticed a major change except that she was more fatigued and sleepy. Yes, the nerve pain episodes had diminished but had not been eliminated. I made the comment that the medication costs a fortune, about $487 for a one month supply, did he have samples? He said he ran out of them, which gave me the impression that his pharmaceutical representative had encouraged him to push this "wonder drug." I told the Neurologist that I actually saw more of an impact from an aspirin, so why bother? Now I got another one of those typical answers, "Well, if you don't want to give her the medication, that's your call." It is really annoying when you can't get one of these doctors to take about three minutes out of their busy schedule to explain why one should stay on the medication they had prescribed. One would assume that they had a medical not financial reason for their selection of a medication. I have a habit of asking questions in order to create a lively debate about the pros and cons of certain situations. It is only then that one can make more informed decisions. Anyhow, since he gave me such a smart answer, I retorted, "Now that you put it this way, can you give me the proper routine to follow." I told him that I had read the warning of not suddenly discontinuing or diminishing the medication. He gave me a piece of paper and wrote down how to reduce it.

I started to diminish the administration of the medicine and meticulously documented my observations on a daily basis. Once she was down to 3 pills a day, I monitored Phyllis' nerve pain. As a result of this, sometimes I temporarily increased the dosage and then returned to the 3 pills a day. I also decided it was high time to find another Neurologist. We did and since then finally found one who can only be described in the most glowing terms. I respect him immensely and he does take the time to discuss different issues. Most importantly, my wife admires him. Both Phyllis and I have been extremely satisfied with his attention and support. What a difference it has been!

Today she is still on this schedule and that approach works great. The only time things went astray was when she was in the hospital in **YEAR 45** because they wouldn't accept my varying dosage routine.

Taking Phyllis to the doctor became increasingly difficult. Getting her ready was quite a job because she no longer could get out of the bed by herself or even dress herself once she was in the wheelchair. Lifting her into the car became much more difficult because she no longer had the strength to put her arms around my neck and hold on. We bought a handicap van allowing her to drive directly into the van with her wheelchair.

YEAR 43:
Patient: Can't feed herself any longer.
Observations: One more for list of "things to do"

At this point her condition had deteriorated to a point where she was no longer able to feed herself. After another one of our cross-country trips it became very clear that this effort was also coming to an end. These trips became increasingly difficult and involved. With the exception of very few items on our "must do list before we can't," we accomplished the majority of the most desirable adventures. That is a major achievement since she still had not reached her "Golden Retirement Age." Is it important to make every effort, you bet it is! Her whole outlook was strengthened by this dedicated effort. Even today she still feels, with my help, she may be able to do one more thing. Remember, one of the most important objectives of a Caregiver should be not to give rise to the muttering of the most dreadful sentence, "I wish I were dead." Stem cell research may come up with the answer every disabled person is looking for, a cure or at least a drastic improvement.

YEAR 44:
Patient: New treatment plan?
Observations: Not appropriate. Turning it down.

Phyllis' left hand locked in a closed position. The Neurologist mentioned a recent new treatment plan which would require quarterly shots, a treatment in the $800 per shot proposition not covered by Medicare.

After discussing it at great length and considering Phyllis' condition, he wasn't sure that the return on that particular investment was of potential value. Based on results with other patients it was very difficult for the providers of this treatment to give the slightest assurance that anything would really change, basically some patients respond favorably and others don't. Isn't that the same as "MAYBE?" The difference between the earlier Neurologists and our current one was so strikingly different. This relationship was on a highly professional level.

Each time I got into a discussion with the previous Neurologist or Urologist they seemed to be incapable of verbalizing specifically what improvement she may be deprived of. I couldn't help but believe that the only ones being deprived of anything were the doctors, specifically their next BMW lease payment. Sometimes I can be quite sarcastic.

The catheter continued to be a troubling contraption and I did everything under the sun to keep infections to a bare minimum.

At this point I had become a more experienced Caregiver and became more aggressive at trying different approaches in order to see how Phyllis would respond. If we were not satisfied with the results, we tried another approach until we saw the desired results. The beneficial part of this exercise was that my services were "free of charge." You may say, "Wow, this is risky!" Well if you feel that way, apparently you have not reached a confidence level necessary to be bold. Do doctors truly know the outcome of specific recommended approaches? Their expertise is guided by the fact that in general terms certain procedures or approaches "generally produce certain results." Do pharmaceutical companies know the result of a certain medication? If they would know, then you wouldn't have all the warnings specifying all the side effects you may encounter. Remember, the caregiver only deals with ONE affliction. There can be no doubt, that this person will be more of an expert in that ONE malady than the most learned doctor who cannot possibly be an expert in the huge variety of medical conditions. The medical field has already been divided into many specialties, but it would be totally counterproductive, at least from an income point of view, to limit the expertise to a very narrow part of the patient population. We already came a long way from the one and only Country Doctor in the TV shows which portray the horse and buggy years.

YEAR 45:
Patient: The Central America research project.
Observations: Risky approach.

Having read that one can live cheaper in Costa Rica, Central America, we thought maybe the business people were on to something about this outsourcing scheme and maybe we should outsource ourselves. Allegedly one can have a home, gardener, nurse and maid all for less than $1,000 per month. Being the eternal optimists, we thought it would be worth making all the arrangements, go through the nightmare of getting on a flight and conduct our research project. We had to find out if what sounded like "being too good to be true" was actually just that. It was an interesting adventure. In order to have any support whatsoever, we would have to live in a compound, surrounded by walls and guards. It may be beautiful inside this walled structure but for freedom loving people like us, it's like agreeing to live in a prison. We checked the whole health care system which was good but a little bit short on certain specialties. We also felt, if for whatever reason, we would have to deal with an emergency, specifically associated with her disease, getting on a flight in her condition could become difficult. Once before, when she was still in better shape and we tried to make reservations on one particular airline out of Saudi Arabia, this particular airline refused to accept her because of potential liabilities. After analyzing all the angles, we both felt it could become an extremely risky proposition. The return trip from Costa Rica became our last airline trip. Phyllis was really stressed out from this exercise and was relieved when we arrived back in familiar surroundings. It became quite obvious that when stress is present, all her problems seem to reappear and increase in intensity.

There was one good benefit as a result of this trip. We were able to buy Neurontin for half the price in Costa Rica as compared to the price we had to pay at the local pharmacy in the USA. This is the same Neurontin, in the same box and exported from the US to Costa Rica. How is that possible? You know that after shipping costs, the pharmaceutical companies still make a profit.

Only three months after our return, she had a seizure during a busy hurricane summer and I was able to nurse her back to the way she was before the seizure. I still had to take her to the Urologist once a month to replace her catheter. At this point she had achieved a record. She was now the person with the longest record of catheter use at this Urology Treatment Center with the least infections. Originally they told us that within 5 to 8 years she would need an operation. By now she was in her 12th year and almost every few months we were told she should undergo the operation. I felt like I was watching a TV program and listened to the same commercial over and over again. The explanation was still the same as the one given for the **YEAR 40** version; nothing had changed. At no time did they test anything which potentially could have shown evolving kidney or bladder problems, nothing! Even without any further knowledge of her condition, the drumbeat for the operation continued. We kept on resisting. Later on you will see why our objections turned out to be the correct approach.

YEAR 46:
Patient: The worst year ever-close to death!
Observations: True 24/7 Caregiving. Stress at its peak.

This became a defining year. We moved into this year with more frequent visits to the primary care physician for her regular visits plus the additional affliction of diabetes. The Ear, Nose and Throat specialist was honored by our visits because she suddenly had frequent hearing problems in her left ear. The Urologist saw us more because of increased occurrences of catheter obstructions. Frequent pain attacks, nerve and plain old pain, made us frequent guests of our Neurologist. From a Caregivers point of view, this created an extremely stressful, worrisome and hectic schedule.

The catheter size was increased to the largest one available but it only temporarily relieved the problem. It was clogged over and over again. Many times it was possible to clear it up by flushing. Unfortunately, the frequency of obstructions increased, diminishing the ability to clear it up. The only alternative was to have the catheter removed and an appointment made to see the Urologist for the insertion of a new one. In light of this, our joint resistance to the operation was labeled as obstinate, uncooperative and potentially damaging to Phyllis' health. It is very hard not to cave in when that much pressure is being applied. The key issue, which kept us from relenting, was the fact that after the suggested operation would be performed, in order to have the catheter inserted through her belly, we were unable to get any assurance that the potential clogging of the catheter would be drastically diminished as compared to having one inserted through the urethra. What was worse, if clogging would occur after the operation, she would have to be taken to the emergency room because my removal of the catheter, so easily done when it is placed in the bladder, was more tricky and could potentially cause an infection around the site. I am sure over time, maybe, this situation could be brought under control but being very skeptical and analyzing the pros and cons, as I always had to do in my previous job as a corporate executive, it just didn't favor the operation.

The hearing problem led to tests and recommendations of a hearing aid and since her speech was impaired, another recommendation for a potential operation. Phyllis was born with a cleft palate and an operation was performed within a year after her birth. This type of an operation, at the time it was performed, was a first. The operation was a success in terms of the capabilities of that era. As she grew up, and for the rest of her life, she had an acceptable speech deficiency. Current medical skills and procedures had improved tremendously and it was felt that they could repair the roof of her mouth and make her speak normally. Why?

Fortunately we received some real common sense recommendations from Phyllis' Ear, Nose and Throat specialist. He said, "No hearing aid, she has an unusual wax buildup and frequent removal should improve the hearing problem." It did! As for the speech problem, his feeling was that her speech deficiency wasn't solely as a result of the cleft palate situation but further impaired by her Multiple Sclerosis, therefore an operation may repair something but resolve nothing.

Her diabetes brought on a new medication to keep glucose levels at an acceptable level. The problem was that even following the treatment plan as stipulated by her doctor didn't prevent sudden wide swings in glucose readings.

Since she was on Neurontin and some additional nerve pain inhibitors, plus a strong dosage of pain killers, it became very difficult to determine what was causing an increasing amount of lethargy. Was it as a result of the frequent high readings of her glucose level, frequent infections in her bladder, the nerve pain killers or a combination of all three?

While all this was going on, her appetite was diminishing and it became very difficult to motivate her to eat and keep her at a sustaining caloric level.

She started to lose weight. All her life she had been a petite 90 pound lady. The fact that she was now losing weight was an extremely troublesome event.

The combination of all the maladies finally reached a very critical state in early September. This happened over the three day Labor Day weekend. Why do these problems always occur at the wrong time? Her temperature shot up to 104.5 degrees and her limbs totally locked up. It was impossible to even move her arms. She was totally incoherent and was rushed to the emergency room.

She had a large bladder stone and the debris which clogged the catheter was as a result of a severe kidney infection. Her right kidney had totally shut down because of an infection the size of a golf ball. Her other organs were ready to call it quits and she had lost 10 pounds. She was in a semi-coma and needed an emergency operation to either relieve her right kidney or remove it altogether.

It was the early afternoon and blood for a transfusion was expected in a few hours so the operation was scheduled for 5PM. A new Urologist took over since her Urologist of many years never checked or anticipated this kidney infection which had been building up. In spite of the warning signs, no tests were ever conducted. What was the reason for this? One can only speculate. From their perspective, we were obstinate people and difficult to deal with.

Due to Phyllis' critical condition, the Urologist told me that we had to make a very important decision. He then painted a very grim and depressing picture. He felt that even if the blood would not arrive in time, the operation had to proceed. He needed my approval. A delay would also increase blood poisoning problems. I was now faced with a decision which could potentially be fatal to the patient. I asked him to give me about half an hour since I wanted to discuss it with my daughter.

Here is the summary of the analysis based on the many questions the Urologist answered to the best of his ability:

1.-Operate at 5PM with blood available. Potential success slightly better than 50%, but not certain.

2.-Operate at 5PM without blood available. Success potential 50/50, could be fatal.

3.-Operate later after blood available. Success potential less than 50%, could be fatal because of the delay.

Delay was a bigger danger than the lack of blood, so we made the decision to proceed with option 2. Thankfully, the blood arrived in time; the operation proceeded and was successful.

We were now faced with the recovery process.

A drainage line was inserted into her right kidney. A PIC line was inserted into her left arm for antibiotics and because she was unable to eat, a PEG tube was inserted into her stomach. She was in the Intensive Care Unit (ICU) and for six days Phyllis was in a semi coma, rarely opening her eyes and not being aware of anything. On the sixth night, some family member was on guard duty. I left the hospital at eleven o'clock. At two in the morning, I received a call to come to the hospital because Phyllis was asking for me. I went immediately and when I arrived, she took my hand and asked me, "What am I doing here?" I started to explain when she interrupted me and said, "Get me out of here!" It was then that I finally knew I would have my honey back.

The following night, I left at midnight and turned the watch over to one of our family members. Around 3AM the family member called to let me know that the nurse had given my wife an injection of morphine because of her severe pain. I went back to the hospital and asked the nurse, "What happened, what severe pain?" She said it was hard for her and my family member to get a clear picture but my wife was pointing to her lower belly. I now got into a lengthy discussion with the nurse. After I found out that the wrong size catheter had been inserted, I told her to remove it immediately because the pain had nothing to do with her bladder but that the balloon had been over inflated in her urethra not in the bladder. I further told her to replace it with the correct catheter. They had inserted a different size, because they didn't have the right size in stock. I knew what had happened based on a previous experience. I told her I had the correct catheters at home, which brought the conversation to the whole subject of hospital rules, something I wasn't about to tackle. She said she couldn't remove the catheter without the doctor's approval. I told her in no uncertain terms to remove it. I said I would take full responsibility for it. She did and the pain disappeared almost instantly. It was then that I realized that making the assumption that all these professionals were skilled and experienced individuals was wishful thinking. Over time I had become an expert regarding **this** patient. This experience only encouraged me to use my expertise and use paid professional assistance when required.

I also realized this revered medical environment was grossly flawed with its strange rules. It is no secret that nurses are responsible for the caring of their patients and held accountable, especially if something goes astray. In spite of this very important burden they have no authority to make important decisions based on their expertise. The general rule is that they must call the doctor, who may or may not be available as expeditiously as the situation may warrant and only then they may make a decision, but GOD forbid, if something goes wrong. With that burden hanging over their heads, I am not surprised at their reluctance to make bold decisions. I finally realized that in the future I would have to take on most of the requirements for my wife's care and may have to handle tough situations, sometimes without the immediate help from medical professionals. While all these doctors have answering services, sometimes, for whatever reason, they cannot respond as expeditiously as you would expect. One has to understand that doctors are human beings who also have priorities.

On day nine, a Friday, still in ICU, I was informed that she would be released. I looked at the doctor and at Phyllis in disbelief. Here is the patient with a drainage tube coming out of her right kidney, a catheter in her urethra, a line into her vein to give her antibiotics twice a day, a feeding tube in her stomach and an oxygen tube in her nose. In addition to that the nurses tested her glucose level several times a day, gave her insulin shots to bring her glucose readings to an acceptable range and her urine had to be checked for any unusual signs, like blood and the degree of clarity. Now they want to release her into my care, when I have to push all these tubes away, just to give her a kiss? Was this a compliment? Had they recognized my expertise? Before my ego bubble could inflate, a nurse told me that insurance companies don't like to pay hospital expenses if they can UNLOAD the patient. They put a lot of pressure on doctors. I told my doctor, the only way I will accept a release is if all the doctors involved and there were four, answer all the questions which I will give to them in writing. I immediately sat down and listed all my questions; I came up with a total of 42 questions, covering issues such as WHAT TO DO, HOW TO DO IT and WHAT TO WATCH OUT FOR. I made one sheet for each doctor. The nurses got on the phone to each doctor and obtained the explanations and answers I had requested.

By two in the afternoon, I had them and I accepted the release. I was overwhelmed and the homecare help I received was bare bones and minimal. I entered everything into the computer, in between paying attention to Phyllis, and playing data entry clerk, eventually got my total schedule with an hourly description of all the things that had to be done and the numerical data I had to check or maintain, including her blood pressure, temperature and glucose level. It went from 7AM to 11PM each and every day for a 17 day period, non-stop, when the pic line was removed. The drainage line from her kidney was not removed until after she had an operation to remove the kidney stone, which occurred 30 days after her release from the hospital. 30 days after that, she was scheduled for another operation when they removed the bladder stone.

In retrospect, while I was overwhelmed, when she was released into my care because I was scared that if I missed one of the many needed procedures, she would suffer the consequences of this nightmarish obsession by insurance companies when greed is more important to them than the medical welfare of a patient, I am actually thankful that they forced me into this situation. I seriously doubt that she would have gotten anywhere near the very detailed and minute by minute attention in the hospital. I became a professional and expert Caregiver.

While I had a hernia from lifting Phyllis in and out of bed and into the wheelchair, it suddenly tore more and I ended up in the emergency room myself, not a pretty picture. During my recovery, I called on friends and family members to help with the lifting until a ceiling lift could be installed. In spite of it all, I have been slowly nursing Phyllis back to an acceptable level, her being comfortable, in spite of all these diverse requirements, is all one can expect. My biggest reward is when she expresses her deep appreciation for all I do for her and that there is no way she would feel at all happy and comfortable without my help. I am not good at handling praise so my response is, "You are just a pain in the ass, I have no choice to do what I am doing" and she retorts with her favorite response, "Jerk!" She smiles at me, we both laugh and I kiss her.

YEAR 47:
Patient: Slow recovery-Eliminate catheter.
Observations: Mostly taking over from doctors.

As a Caregiver, your never know when your workload will increase. I unexpectedly became the caregiver for my mother when her health suddenly took a turn for the worse. A Caregiver has to learn to role with the punches and maintain his composure. It required some adjustments to my schedule and getting used to a new routine.

This year Phyllis showed some more improvements. After the right kidney recovered fully and the bladder was functioning better, I told the Urologist that I felt it would be in Phyllis' best interest to remove the catheter altogether and rely on a combination of serenity pads and fitted briefs. He pointed out that as long as I was willing to do the extra work, give her a regular dosage of water, acidifier, a sustaining mild antibiotic and watch everything very carefully, he had no objections. Not caving in to the drumbeat about the operation to have the catheter placed into my wife's belly and "decommission" the bladder had finally paid off. He scheduled several cat scans during the year to make sure the kidney and the bladder were getting better and stronger. Once he was satisfied that this Caregiver was performing to perfection, he scheduled yearly visits. The caloric amount of nutritional supplements fed through her feeding tube was modified twice during the year after she had gained her weight back. The Neurologist agreed for me to make changes to her medication program based on my observations, either increase it or decrease it depending on specific conditions. Glucose levels started to be less erratic and we had to rely less and less on insulin to bring things under control. During this period we developed a relationship of mutual respect with all the physicians who were part of her care team.

YEAR 48:
Patient: Greatly improved-Better than 2 years ago.
Observations: The greatest reward

In the early part of the year, Phyllis had a PEG tube change, a procedure done in the hospital. Her recovery was proceeding and she was feeling better and better. A Dermatologist and a Wound Care Specialist were added to the array of my medical consultants. By now she had reached a point of being 95% bedridden. Maintaining her skin was important in order to prevent potential infections. In some areas it was protected by DuoDerm patches. The skin problems around her feeding tube were treated with an antibacterial cream and covered with a PolyMem Silver Pad. Her glucose readings indicated that no further insulin was required, as a matter of fact, her glucose readings had returned to that of a person without diabetes. While her voice is weak, with a little bit of effort, we manage. For the transportation VAN we use a "Speech Enhancement System" which amplifies her weak and subdued voice so that she can communicate with me while I am driving. She is in better shape than in **Year 45**, when she almost passed away. Her medication has been drastically reduced.

All the doctors have now complimented me for my care and attention and have expressed amazement as to how well Phyllis has recovered. One of the physicians said, he would love to hire me because I am better than all the people he has or ever had working for him.

While a compliment such as this is nice, still my biggest reward and satisfaction is the fact that the minute I show up or sit next to my wife, she always smiles. She has such a beautiful smile! Can't beat LOVE!

YEAR 49:
Patient: Improvements wiped out.
Observations: Professional failures!

The year started on a happy note, but by the end of the second month, the PEG tube got totally clogged. One would assume this to be a minor problem. Wrong! NO, Dead wrong! I made an appointment and took my wife to the Gastroenterologist, who had replaced the tube several times, and told him we had a problem with the PEG tube. His answer was, "I only put the tubes in and take them out." That answer suited me fine and I came up with a simple and logical response. I told him, fine – "take it out and put a new one in." His answer baffled me. He said, "she has an infection around the tube, therefore it has to heal first before I can do anything, besides it has to be scheduled and it will take time." I was shocked to say the least. I asked him, "You mean to tell me that there is no specialty that can unclog a PEG tube?" The answer was, "I don't know of anyone." My amazement was growing and I asked him again, "You mean to tell me that there is no "Roto-Router" type service for a PEG tube?" He said again he wasn't sure. I retorted again and said, "You mean to tell me that science has progressed to the point that a sewer line can be unclogged but the medical profession hasn't figured out how to unclog a PEG tube or lacking that, insert a new tube and treat the infection with antibiotics?" He did answer and told me to see her Primary

Care Physician. On the way out, I told him, "Thank God our soldiers have better physicians when they are wounded otherwise they would all come back in body bags." He wasn't quite pleased with my comment. For this fantastic service, he still collected his co-payment. This was the last time we saw that doctor. I called the Primary Care Physician for an appointment and we were able to see him immediately.

The Primary Care Physicians immediate comment was, "Why are you coming to me, I don't know how to handle this," but after a brief conversation, he volunteered to check with the hospital where he is accredited. I told him, "if the Gastroenterologist I just left is their doctor and he doesn't know what to do, why would we want to go to that hospital?" He agreed and called another hospital approved by her insurance. The X-Ray department told him to send her there. I immediately went to that hospital and they took her in. After about ½ hour, a technician was driving her wheelchair out and he was all wet. I looked at him and asked him what had happened. They had attempted to clear the obstruction by pushing water under pressure through the tube. He did exactly what I had done, before I took her to the doctor. The end result was a repeat of my own experience, it didn't work. I told them, "I thought you had some device that would go through and basically drill out whatever had clogged the tube, not do what I had done."

So they basically said they can't do anything – sorry! I asked them, "What is she going to do, just starve to death?" (In time I found out that "YES" there is a specialty handling issues such as these, but her insurance didn't cover it. That issue was never presented to me and as a result I was not given the choice or opportunity to pay for it out my pocket and prevent the misery that this hospital put my wife and me through. Recently there has been talk about "death panels" associated with the Health Care Reform legislation – maybe they existed all along, we just didn't know! I called her Primary Care Physician and he told me to take her to the emergency room. I did, but I couldn't figure out what they would be able to do, since their own department gave up.

Now the nightmare really started. We had already lost a whole day, she had no food or liquid and I was now informed that the earliest another Gastroenterologist could see her was in 2 days, meaning, she would not be fed for another two days. The hospital put her on an IV. I never left my wife. I observed their routine and realized that the knowledge base and competence of the ICU nurses varies extensively. The minus side wins. I had many discussions with them, pointing out many flaws. Obviously, I was viewed as a total pain, not someone who knew their business better then they ever hoped to achieve. It was only in week two of her stay in the hospital that I finally managed to be accepted for my expertise.

The Gastroenterologist showed up as scheduled. He looked at her PEG tube and came to the brilliant conclusion that the tube had to come out. Since he came to the room with nothing, except his hospital coat and the stethoscope around his neck, I asked him when he intended to change the tube. Now I had a brand new experience of incompetence. He said, "I am taking it out right now while I am here, I am not coming back." I said, "You don't have another tube to put in and if you take it out, the stomach acid will just pour out and burn her belly...." He interrupted me and said, "You may be right, but the hole will close after I pull the tube out" and he proceeded to pull it out before I finished my sentence, "…. since it may take a number of days before the hole will close, if ever." He left with no instructions for the hospital doctor other than to do wound care and limit the stomach acid from pouring out.

I called her Primary Care Physician but he was not accredited at this hospital, so he was not in a position to do anything. Have you ever had the feeling that you were dropped off in a location 2000 miles from nowhere and couldn't turn to anybody for help? Well, I felt I had been set adrift in a boat without a paddle in the middle of the Pacific Ocean. Fortunately, a lady doctor on the night shift was more human and I finally was able to discuss this whole issue with her. She brought in the hospital surgeon but he said he couldn't put a tube in because it was infected and he didn't want to make an incision in a secondary place for the same reason. I was getting more and more disgusted because it really appeared that they just refused to do anything. My frustration bubbled over when I repeated my departing comment to the first Gastroenterologist about our wounded soldiers. This surgeon's reaction was the same. If looks could have killed I would have been flat on my back. The lady doctor then recommended TPN (Total Parenteral Nutrition) for my wife, because anything fed through her mouth came right out of the hole in her belly. In essence, she could not retain anything in her stomach. On day 5, after inserting a PIC line, they finally put her on TPN. While she received nutrition, a new roller coaster ride started. Her diabetes re-appeared big time. Her glucose level suddenly reached higher levels than what she ever had before and she now seemed to go from a very sleepy state to almost semi- coma. She was getting four (4) to five (5) shots of insulin a day. In addition, insulin was injected into the TPN bags in order to somewhat level out her glucose readings. The wound care people attempted to get the burn on her belly under control which now covered an area of 6 by 6 inches and the burn looked like a blow torch had been applied to her belly. I took pictures for our records. I asked the lady doctor if she would call a specific doctor and request him to come to the hospital to look at my wife's belly in order to get another opinion. This was a physician who had dealt with my son in his darkest hours. I had gained a tremendous respect for his professionalism and inventiveness. He agreed and two days later showed up. He immediately recognized me which surprised me. He started to study Phyllis' wound carefully and came up with an idea to fill the hole in her belly with surgical glue, something he said he had never done before because it really wasn't intended for that purpose, but he asked me if I would agree for an experiment. I told him that it was the first smart approach I had heard in that hospital, at least we would find out if we had a winner.

The following day he came back with an assistant. They cleaned the wound and then applied the glue in an attempt to seal the hole and avoid any more spillage of stomach acid. It worked for about 4 days but then it began to disintegrate, something it was supposed to do. Before he left the room, he pulled me aside and asked me to bring my wife to his office as soon as she was released from the hospital.

Now two weeks of no progress began. The glucose excursions didn't settle down to a sensible pattern and the administrative staff started talking to me about my wife being transferred to another institution, a skilled nursing facility and hospice care. I refused. I told them she will only be released into my care and no nursing home, especially hospice care, because that would be a kiss of death. They brought in their big guns telling me I cannot take care of her because it would involve around the clock attention. When they wanted to proceed with their approach, I refused. I had her bundled up, put in her power wheelchair and brought her down to my van. I signed the release papers and took her home. In the meantime, I arranged home delivery for the TPN and had the providers change the set-up to a portable battery operated pump so that this process was not interrupted.

A nurse from the organization that supplied the TPN came to my home and taught me the tricks of the trade, which was mind boggling. I documented the whole process, step by step (39 steps) and then had a dry run with the nurse supervising me until I was able to handle everything flawlessly (See Appendix C for the step by step description). I was more familiar with all the other requirements but again the stress level was very high and the fact that I could only sleep an hour here and there wasn't very helpful. I muddled through; however I realized that I had to find another way to handle her nutrition since continuing with TPN was not sustainable. Wound care was very difficult because of the high glucose readings. I tried to make an appointment with the physician friend of ours and his office staff told me that he didn't accept my wife's insurance and that they wouldn't make an appointment. I then called his nurse who got him on the phone and he said, forget the office, come in.

When we arrived, the receptionist was real snippy. I am sure you will understand that under these circumstances I was not in a very cooperative mood. I told her to just call his nurse and tell her that we are here.

He brought us into one of his well equipped rooms and had the nurse clean the wound thoroughly. Then he said, "pay attention, I will show you how to handle things in the future and you will never run into another clogged PEG tube." He inserted a size 24 catheter, blew up the balloon, anchored the catheter to her belly so it would not slip in and then re-bandaged her belly. He said, "have the TPN removed and from now change the catheter when required. If you have a problem, come see me and I will help you." He gave me some supplies and wished me luck. He didn't accept any payment and said what had happened to her was an outrage and he was certain that with dedicated care I would be able to restore her belly to normal. Since then I have changed her feeding tube four times without a problem. What is unbelievable is that the Gastroenterologist contended he couldn't do anything until the wound was totally healed and then only in a hospital setting and at a cost that would choke a mule. This certainly gives you a real insight about the shortcomings of our health care system.

When I got home, I called the nurse who had helped me with the TPN setup and asked her if she could pull the PIC line and terminate the TPN deliveries. I would now start feeding her through the catheter and resume the feeding as was done before this incident. No sooner had the TPN been terminated, the glucose gyrations began to slow down and within half a year, I finally got her off insulin again. Her Primary Care Physician set up visits by different specialists like a nurse for wound care, a speech therapist and others. In short order, I settled on the Wound Care nurse and none of the others since I didn't see much purpose or hope. The Wound Care nurse started to come once a week to check on my wound care routine and the progress I was making. She also was responsible for changing the catheter in her bladder once a month. Over time, I tried many new approaches to the wound care effort and finally saw the wound go down in size from the 6 by 6 inch burn to the size of a quarter. The dedication and constant attention paid off and she began to improve and regain her positive spirit.

I did contact an attorney, a gentleman who had been a doctor and decided to study law. I presented him with all the records, pictures and documentation which were extensive since I had been at the hospital the whole time making many notes and recording all my observations. I asked him if I had a case to file a malpractice suit against the doctor who pulled the PEG tube. The answer was YES, BUT!!! He asked, "During your 3 weeks in the hospital, did any of the doctors give you any hint that they were appalled by the performance of the Gastroenterologist?" I said, "No they didn't in spite of the fact that I had raised many probing questions. All responses by any medical professional, doctor, nurse or aide were very evasive." He said, "This could and would become a very involved case. Relying on local resources would be of questionable value since they would not be very cooperative. He would have to fly doctors in from other states and the costs would climb quite a bit. While the case was quite compelling, he felt a win may be a loss in the long run and he suggested that I make a business decision." I did and decided to forget the whole issue and concentrate on getting my wife's ugly wound restored to normal.

One would assume that this particular experience was enough for right now. One tries to regain confidence and move on. We were not that lucky. Only 2 months after having my wife released from the hospital, she started to complain again about pain in one tooth. Having had previous experiences with MS induced toothaches we resorted to an earlier treatment plan. When we didn't seem to make any headway, I took her to her dentist. He took x-rays, but couldn't find a reason why she would have any pain. Specifically since the tooth she was complaining about was a false tooth, root canal work had been performed and there was no nerve. The dentist said, the fact that she felt a pain in that general vicinity may be possible, but he didn't see anything which would potentially cause it. He was familiar with our previous experience of treating a nerve on the left side of her face. When I told him that we went through that process already, he recommended a specialist and made the appointment.

We took the x-rays with us, but the specialist decided to take x-rays of her whole mouth. He couldn't find anything that was obvious and said he wanted to take some time studying it and then come up with a treatment plan. She was to come back in a week. In the meantime, I called the neurologist, explained her problem and he suggested a step by step increase in her current pain medication. By the time our appointment for the dental specialist arrived, the pain started to subside and my wife dispatched me to the dentist alone to listen and discuss his treatment plan. In **YEAR 39,** I offered a warning regarding potential scams being perpetrated by dentists. When I went to see this gentleman, I didn't expect anything but a very professional review of her condition and his recommendation. When I arrived, the receptionist escorted me to a nicely furnished conference room which was equipped with a viewer for x-rays. Pretty soon the dentist showed up with his file and placed all the x-rays on the viewer. He handed me a proposal in a nice cover and started to explain the composition of her mouth which was mostly false teeth and bridges, sprinkled with a few real ones. I thought to myself, I don't really need this reminder, since I paid dearly for the previous dental work. Being an extremely curious individual, I couldn't help but take a brief glimpse at the right hand lower part of the proposal which had a number in excess of ten thousand dollars. With a pointer, he showed me why certain nerves could potentially cause the pain. It was his professional opinion that the best thing to do was to remove all her teeth and replace them with a new set of dentures. He stated in very positive terms, that once this procedure had been completed and should she encounter any further pain in the future, we would now have the assurance that the pain was not related to the teeth. Pointing to the x-ray, I questioned him about the lack of any infection and in spite of it, would it not be a more prudent approach to treat her with antibiotics first before resorting to this draconian approach of pulling all the teeth out. While I was extremely polite and calm, he now lectured me that he was the dentist and I really was not qualified to properly read the x-rays. In spite of this shot, I responded by saying that I wasn't questioning his competence or expertise, I just offered what I felt was a more logical approach to proceed. As I said earlier, the approach her Neurologist had recommended seemed to be working, but I didn't even mention this to him. I thanked him for his advice, paid for the consultation and told him, I would discuss it with my wife and let him know of our decision.

What surprised me was a call from her dentist saying that the specialist had called him and he strongly urged us to consider his recommendation. I had always had great respect for our dentist and really liked him, suddenly that sent a chill down my spine.

Within a month, the treatment plan recommended by her neurologist paid off and the pain disappeared and hasn't come back since then. She still has her beautiful smile with the same assortment of teeth she had before.

In ending the description of the 49 year progression of a Caregiver/ Patient relationship, it is also important to understand that my wife has never taken any medication intended for Multiple Sclerosis. Before her diagnosis, in **YEAR 20,** no medication could have been offered anyhow, even if it existed. After the diagnosis, many times she was offered medications which were portrayed as potentially being beneficial to her MS without any assurances they actually would be. This documented description of a 49 year progression of MS must be viewed in that light. It does not prove anything pro medication or against medication treatment plans, all it proves is that here is one patient that progressed from perfectly normal to a quadriplegic state over a long period of time. She is living a very happy, fruitful life and today is still capable of planning for more fun experiences as long as her Caregiver husband doesn't give up, something she knows will never happen voluntarily.

Orphan Disease

An orphan disease is a rare disease. It is one that affects only a relatively small number of individuals, usually defined as people in the US. Any financial investment into the research effort for diseases labeled as such would not provide a very favorable return on the investment. If some medication or cure could be found, the cost of such medication or procedure would be prohibitive. It would be highly unlikely that most people affected by these diseases would be able to pay for it. Would insurance companies cover it? It is hard to imagine that they would, but then who really knows.

There are thousands of these diseases. Let's use some of the numbers that are being thrown around. A disease which afflicts about 150,000 worldwide multiplied by a minimum of 6,000 identified rare diseases equals about 900 million people who the pharmaceutical industry has determined don't deserve much attention, unless they can rake you over the coals. They can identify many diseases, like "RLS or restless leg syndrome," which is not a rare disease. I am sure even you have run into it when you were just tired, stressed out or nervous. They can spend millions of dollars in TV advertising to sucker you into buying the "CURE." There are other rare diseases in our country, such as malaria, typhoid and cholera, which are more widespread in third world countries. They will only receive attention when something unique happens, like the case of a tuberculosis patient several years ago who managed to slip in and out of the US.

In 1983, the US Orphan Drug Act was passed. It provides tax incentives and a seven year exclusive marketing umbrella for drugs developed for these rare diseases. The pharmaceutical companies have taken advantage of this law and developed certain drugs. While the Orphan Drug Act may have its origin based on a noble intent, the pharmaceutical industry saw this as a for profit opportunity. When greed enters the picture, the well being of potential patients drops to the bottom of the barrel when it comes to developing priorities. Am I unduly negative? Look at the reality. When grants are given, private or governmental, those who completed their paperwork successfully will, if at all possible translate that into a perpetual income stream. Just human nature! Research into many areas which may produce the much touted "CURE" can be easily justified. Nowadays, it seems more and more diseases are either identified or invented. You may view this comment as extremely cynical or you may not be inclined to accept reality; sometimes living in a dream world is more comfortable. The success of the efforts to develop disease fighting drugs is shown in improving statistics by the drug companies. The following expression fits: "Figures don't lie, liars can figure!" Here are some other statistics. In 1996, 108,000 Americans died in hospitals from adverse reactions to FDA approved drugs. This is the 4th leading cause of death in our country, enough to scare me. That same year 2.2 million had adverse reactions to FDA approved drugs. You and I have heard stories about our fabulous medical research. The USA is 37 in the ranking of best health care, right on top of the third world countries. We have heard much about a slogan "no child left behind." I am not sure what this slogan is attempting to define because the USA is the second worst industrialized nation in newborn fatality rates, obviously they were left behind. The worst are three nations with an equal rating that were under the domination of the former Soviet Union. Finally, our mortality rate (2006) is in line with the industrialized world at around 8.26 deaths per thousand of the population and has improved very little since 2003.

Another item which has been drilled into our minds is "smoking will be dangerous to your health." I don't doubt for a minute that it may be to some, but to state it as an all inclusive fact flies in the face of reality. The INCAS, South American Indians, have been smoking "Nicotiana Rustica," a tobacco leaf with a nicotine content of twice our tobacco. They have been dying of old age. In their jungle environment they didn't have to deal with exhaust fumes from their limos. It really should raise a question in your mind, are you truly being given the truth and nothing but the truth. Do you still believe I am a cynic?

Another approach is to quote surveys to justify whatever they want to sell you on. Some years back I received a telephone call asking me to participate in a survey. It was about migraine headaches. Since I am fortunate enough not to suffer from this affliction, I only made a comment that if someone had constant migraine headaches, I wouldn't be surprised if eventually they would blow their brains out. After the Ha, Ha, the survey was over. Sometime after that, at least several years later, I read one of these medical reports quoting surveys and it was determined that people with migraine headaches have a higher tendency of committing suicide! I have no idea if this is true or not; the migraine headache afflicted people I know are still among the living.

A number of drugs have been developed for MS patients. They are very expensive and I cannot help but question if they actually provide the relief the pharmaceutical companies have portrayed. I am sure there are patients who will take an exception to my comment. All I can say, if it works for them, either by their strong belief in the medication or for real, bless them.

Health Insurance
(The ugly truth)

There is one major exception regarding the heading of this section. The Medicare related health insurance offered by a number of Health Insurance companies as of this writing can only be described in positive terms. They truly go out of their way to be helpful and because of the Medicare association are much clearer as to what is and what is not covered. It is ironic that so many uninformed retired people are opposed to government run health care because they don't want them to touch their MEDICARE, which is a popular program. Their uninformed opposition would deprive people under 65 and the uninsured of the same benefits, I really doubt that this is their true intention.

The views expressed regarding the new Health Reform legislation ranges from extremely negative to extremely positive. Eventually, I am sure we will settle down somewhere closer to the middle. In the beginning of this book I explain that as a Caregiver for over 24 years I approach things with a complete positive attitude and the negative things are for your awareness and knowledge. When I encounter negative insurance issues, I do my very best to be factual and not resort to emotional editorials, however, regarding this particular issue, it is virtually impossible, probably totally impossible, to not have an emotional reaction to what I, and most likely you, will encounter…the reaction is ANGER. There really is no other way to say it.

Like everything else in this book, the following are absolute facts about the industry and my experiences. Before I became a caregiver I was a high level computer professional for 33 years. As such, I had many opportunities to visit computer installations of Insurance companies. I also had many conversations with programmers from that industry. If anyone wants to know where all the skeletons are buried, ask a programmer who developed the code for a company, since they are truly the only ones who know the inner workings and intent of any system. Again, this is awareness and knowledge...in some cases, anger (controlled) crawls in when you are dealing with a multitude of hypocrisy, autocratic policies and political absurdity.

Unfortunately, Insurance does NOT mean Assurance. Yes, the facts are true.

Most people assume that insurance is there to provide relief to stricken people when in need. Since the vast majority of people covered by insurance rarely ever file a claim, the view and general concept of "insurance" is that the cost is spread over a large segment of the population thus providing all people with a safety net when some unexpected or rare calamity hits. Well, how do the insurance companies see it? Currently the insurance companies view it as an income stream, like a broken ATM endlessly dispensing money to their CEO's, other top executives, board members and some small amount to their shareholders. Unfortunately, in our country, the insurance industry is not prohibited from cherry picking the cream of the crop, people who are deemed to be somewhat less likely to get sick, and as a result, represent pure profit. Those that may have some kind of a medical problem, based on the insurance company's interpretation of the individual's application, are discouraged through high premiums or found to be "unacceptable," for whatever reason. Insurance companies have basically become the opposite of Loan Sharks and Credit Card companies. They (the insurance industry) only want people who pay their premiums and hopefully never use their services. Loan Sharks and Credit Card companies want only those who have a hard time paying back loans so that interest rates and fees rocket to astronomical heights. The government endorsed loan sharks, the bank credit card entities, call people who pay their total charges on time each and every month "DEADBEATS!"

When dealing with anything associated with your health, be it good, bad or indifferent, follow one cardinal rule; keep it as private as humanly possible. Also keep that information limited to a very small circle, guard it like you are protecting national security secrets. The most "meaningful warning" is the one given to soldiers who may be captured by our enemies, "give name, rank and serial number," period!

The point is, never volunteer any information to insurance companies or their agents. Answer questions correctly, provided you have the correct answer and never speculate about your condition or offer opinions.

Unfortunately, the insurance industry has evolved into the most predatory and intrusive industry in our country. If you think the NSA (National Security Agency) is a data mining expert, you are totally mistaken. The insurance industry leaves the NSA in the dust.

Keeping your medical condition as private as humanly possible in order to diminish whatever real or factitious detrimental health information may be floating around, is extremely important. Under those conditions you are a good candidate to obtain insurance at what I will call "reasonable" rates. Since insurance companies do extensive spying, an unfounded comment by someone in your neighborhood such as, "I heard that this person may have been treated for some malady" could result in a higher rate and a question mark on your record.

Should you then suddenly develop some unexpected and severe malady which requires the insurance company or entity to lay out more than they felt was acceptable, they will send out investigators to uncover anything about you which they could use to deny, delay or accuse you of defrauding the company in order to diminish or even deny payment for your claim. The basic rule by insurance companies is to deny, delay and then use their resources to fight against you with their attorneys. That principle, in spite of the fact that many issues that end up before a jury and may on the surface go against them, are winners for them. Most people will usually cave against that onslaught of this powerful organization. That is a winner for them! If a lengthy process goes against them, in an industry with huge financial resources, delay means interest on the money and that is a winner. If you think oil companies are making insane profits, look at the insurance industry. They make huge profits but are the biggest doomsayers known to mankind. Their true financials are rarely mentioned by the media and they certainly don't advertise it.

If you feel you only want what is rightfully yours, they will brand you as a thief and a crook. This attitude by the insurance industry has evolved over the last 35 years and is purely driven by greed and corruption. They consider ALL policyholders thieves and treat them as such. This then creates a "get even" attitude by many policy holders from which the wonderful people of the insurance industry need to protect you, otherwise premiums would have to be raised even higher. You lose, they win!

Battling against insurance companies is a battle between terrorists and freedom fighters. While you feel you are dealing with terrorists, the insurance company labels you, the policyholder the terrorist. You, and maybe your attorney, are the freedom fighters. As you can see, they always try to be the victims. Unfortunately, we really have no choice but to deal with them. Because of the way they have influenced politicians with huge infusions of cash, we now have all kinds of laws protecting insurance companies that don't make any sense. For instance, it is mandatory to have insurance for your home if you have a mortgage. This coverage is defined by insurance double-talk policies not just to cover your mortgage but a number of other provisions or liability coverage when someone may break their leg on your property. That scenario then becomes another battle. Should this be covered by someone's health insurance or the homeowner's policy? Car Insurance is required in order to get your tag or plate. Here too you have a built in conflict with your health insurance, another battleground to be fought over by attorneys. If it would be covered through a general pool covered by gas taxes, all these different provisions of uninsured versus insured would disappear. The insurance companies have never battled for mandatory health insurance, because that would blow their ability to confuse, divide and deny. With health insurance you have an option, you either have it (basically can pay a premium) or you don't because you just can't afford it. For those who are dead set against "Universal Health Care" I have this question. Who do you think is paying for the nearly 50 million people who have no health care coverage when in need? If **you** are covered by **your** own health insurance policy or through **your** employer and **pay taxes, you** are paying through higher premiums and increased taxes for the health care of those that go bankrupt or just cannot pay or get services through Medicaid. If you think the medical profession and hospitals are taking the position "well, the poor sucker just can't pay, let's forget it," **wake up!** Hopefully you don't fall out of your bed when you wake up and break your back, it may not be covered. **Read that explanation again –**

maybe it will sink in! Furthermore, if you are so vehemently opposed to Universal Health Care, why are you paying hard earned money in taxes to the privileged politicians you elect so that they have "Universal Health Care?" Does that make any sense? These are the same people who can't figure out how to set up a health care system like the ones in the rest of the industrialized world and many third world countries! Is the money the insurance companies place under the pillows of your elected officials putting too much pressure on their non- existing brains?

The customer service people you usually deal with at insurance companies are probably the loveliest people–they work so hard and their lives would be so much simpler if they could actually provide customer service – but they work for an insurance company – an institution that ties the hands of caring employees and threatens them with dismissal if they step out of the box. I actually feel sorry for these people. They really need the money and all the good employers took off to find greener (cheaper) pastures to reward foreign productive people for pennies on the dollar. The only choice left is to accept a job from the **DEVIL**.

How about the applications for insurance coverage? Have you ever filled out an application for any insurance coverage? It is not one sheet; it is almost a booklet with many questions about health issues you have not experienced and probably never heard anything about them before, worse yet, you may not have a clue what they are talking about. These questionnaires are the most intrusive ever invented. You will always find this question. "Do you have high blood pressure or have you had high blood pressure?" One of these days you will have to answer if you INTEND to have high blood pressure, and if you were to have it, would you do something about it? If for some reason you encountered high blood pressure for any reason or due to an activity and decided to lower it with a glass of grapefruit juice, do you have high blood pressure? Not in your mind! If you go to the doctor and based on a few readings he or she diagnoses you as a potential candidate for high blood pressure and prescribes medication as a precautionary action, you are a marked person and must answer "YES" on the questionnaire forever. If you are under the impression that once you take the medication and your blood pressure is normal and you are yawning all the time, you still must answer "YES" to the question.

Why? Because sometime in the future you may encounter a serious and potentially costly health repair job, even unrelated to your blood pressure, one that may impact the profitability of the insurance carrier, you will be dropped like a hot potato because you now became one of those crooks who falsified the application and they have to protect all the other policy holders from felons like you. They even check your credit report. Why? You may think, if you don't pay, they will cancel you anyhow, so why do they want to know your credit history. The answer to that is as follows. "Studies have shown that on average people who handle their finances responsibly are more responsible in general; they are a better risk." Freely translated, "we can make a higher profit because our operating costs will be lower."

You may feel a conversation between you and your agent is privileged information. It isn't! Don't ever express a potential fear of a health problem because someone in the family six generations back died of a stroke, somehow that will find its way into insurance records and will bite you where it hurts.

Even when you see a doctor, it is quite common that people are misdiagnosed. Sometimes it is just very hard to come up with the correct diagnosis. Medicine is an art, not a science. Unbelievable things happen in the broad category of HEALTH CARE. Add to that carelessness. If you think I am exaggerating, then how is it possible that the left leg of a patient got amputated when the right leg was the problem?

There is also another potential for misdiagnosis, it is erroneous or improper coding of your insurance claim. There may come a time when you are confronted with having a disease, affliction or condition you never heard of. Sometimes this misdiagnosis will be used either as a reason to deny certain insurance, raise the rate or give the insurance company some mystical reason to cancel an existing policy. A misdiagnosis, even after it has been proven to be erroneous, will be retained in insurance records. When a misdiagnosis has occurred, have it properly documented. This is something that is not easily done because it is rare for the doctor who misdiagnosed it (thanks to the legal profession) to provide you with a written retraction explaining why it was wrong and based on what subsequent analysis.

Somehow you must get it, even if it is in the form of a letter from you to the doctor stating the fact that it was misdiagnosed. Unless he proves otherwise in a written denial letter, it can always be used as your proof. Reason: A misdiagnosis is kept by insurance companies and shared. Any official retraction will basically be ignored by the insurance company. In case of a serious legal confrontation such documentation, as described, will definitely be of value.

Keep in mind one very important factor. Many physicians have to resort to the use of "billing services" to facilitate the doctor's nightmarish claim submissions process. In this area, organizations range from ethical to totally unscrupulous. They may truly miscode your claim unintentionally, basically make a mistake, but some are totally unethical and do it purposely in order to achieve a higher return for the physician or themselves. In the end, you, the patient, or your caregiver representative will be the losers no matter what. What is worse, you are given very limited or cryptic information to make any challenge exceedingly difficult.

You may look at this as "so what" as long as it doesn't cost me more, who cares. There is usually nothing you could do about it unless it is outright fraud, like you haven't seen a doctor in years and you get statements from the insurance company that your claim has been processed.

Sometimes it comes to light, when you either change health insurance or you are applying for life insurance and you are either turned down because of an ailment you were unaware you had or you are rated up because of some unknown affliction. Insurance companies rarely will modify a rating once it is in their records. They are right and you, who knows better, is wrong.

In light of this, one would assume that insurance companies would want to have you deeply involved in the claims submitted to them in your behalf. Wrong!

They are quite happy in creating the illusion that they take this heavy burden off your back during these troubled moments. They will deal with all those people who are charging these excessive fees, like doctors and hospitals and then when your policy comes up for renewal they play the victim.

Explanation of benefits is not very informative. Most will tell you the amount of your liability for a procedure. It will list the provider's name that billed, but it portrays a confusing picture as to what the insurance company was billed, what it actually paid and how they arrived at your liability. I am not talking about the published and standard co-payments.

It would be so simple to show the date, the provider and the specific service billed. Instead, they show a bunch of codes which are meaningless to you. Key information should be provided such as what was specifically billed to the insurance company, how much they actually paid, was it based on a contract and most importantly if certain items were denied. What was the reason, especially if they suddenly show up as your responsibility.

They really don't want for you to get too involved and ask silly questions, like why should I pay for a 5 day stay in the hospital when I was there only 2 days? Oops, someone made a mistake??? They are perfectly happy with you, the patient clinging on to the notion that "I am covered by insurance" therefore it really is not my problem, "it is something between them and the provider."

Wrong! No matter what, it's your cost. By the way when you signed some of the forms, either at the doctor's office or at the hospital, you agreed to pay them in the event the insurance company didn't, for whatever reason. Even if the provider didn't follow its contractual obligations with the insurance company, you are liable. If you are prearranging a procedure, find out up front what the charge will be from the doctor, the hospital and the insurance company. You are not wasting your time by talking to all of them, even if they brand you a pain.

Insurance companies are only interested in healthy people, therefore the caregivers are not only faced with the need to pay attention to their patient, they are probably facing expenses which are not covered by insurance, at least if the insurance company can get away with it. Even healthy people who pay their premiums and, as such, feel protected, see their insurance go up year after year and they haven't even filed a claim. Why? Health care costs keep on climbing but if we don't file claims, why don't the premiums get invested and increase in value to be available for a rainy day?

I did an analysis when I retired at age 56. I changed my health insurance to the highest deductible I was able to get. I placed 50% of that amount into an interest bearing account and then deposited the insurance premium that I had saved by the reduction in coverage into this account each month. I paid all my medical expenses out of this account. When Medicare finally kicked in, I had a significant savings account. What a bonus! Why can't the insurance companies do that? GREED!

The doctor's practice also has to deal with insurance companies, blood sucking entities who make life miserable with rules designed to enrich the insurance industry at the expense of not only you, but also the medical profession. They have no mercy! Have you ever seen the listings the doctor is supposed to use when coding whatever he or she is doing in order to process a claim for payment? In reviewing the list, I got dizzy. It is insane! If the office files a claim and accidentally reverses a set of numbers, payment is delayed, sometimes for months. In essence, the doctor is between the rock and the hard place, even the best has to cut corners in order to make a decent living and repay his huge debt. When you leave the doctor's office, you are done, but his nightmare with insurance plans isn't over yet.

Here is a sampling of definitions to which the doctor's office has to code ailments. Each item has a specific code number attached. I am sure different insurance companies have their own versions and probably their own interpretations, making this process a nightmare for the doctors.

I found a total of 522 definitions. I am only showing a sampling (9.2%) to demonstrate the complexity.

Blood RelatedMental/	Nervous Disorders	Musculoskeletal
Agranulocytosis	Alcohol abuse, unspecified	Arthritis
Anemia, unspecified	Anorexia nervosa	Backache, unspecified
Aplastic anemia, unspec.	Anxiety state	Bursitis
Blood chemistry	Bipolar disorder, unspec.	Cervicalgia (neck pain)
Chronic lymphadenitis	Bulimia nervosa	Chest pain/pressure
Coagulation profile	Chronic alcoholism	Cramp in limb
Folate deficiency anemia	Depression	Enthesopathy
Iron deficiency anemia	Drug dependence, unspecified	Forearm
Lymphadenitis	Headache, tension	Lumbago
Mesenteric, nonspecific	Impotence/frigidity	Myalgia/myositis
Other B12 deficiency anemia	Paranoid state, unspecified	Neuralgia/neuritis
Other coagulation defect	Psychogenic pain, unspec.	Osteoporosis
Pernicious anemia	Schizophernia	Pelvic region/thigh
Primary thrombocytopenia	Senile dementia	Rheumatism
Secondary thrombocytopenia	Vascular dementia & depression	Spasm, muscle
Thrombocytopenia	Tobacco dependence	Spondylitis

As I said before, the insurance companies rake the physicians over the coals. You may be under the misguided impression that if the charge, as an example is $200.00 and your co-payment is $20, that the insurance company pays $180 to the physician. Fat chance!

If you run a business and each time you are chiseled down by these greedy and inefficient bureaucrats, what would that do to your attitude? It certainly can't be a cherished moment when they see their financial reward. It is important for you to understand the environment. Personally I feel many physicians don't show enough imagination. Defensive measures would be labeled "shady" by the insurance industry; I would call it "survival." In all of my years of dealing with multiple physicians, I only met one who somehow managed to stay ahead of the insurance nightmare. This physician was a refugee from a foreign country. Maybe when he interpreted the rules something got lost in the translation.

And now I want to give you a real example of how an insurance company rakes you, the patient, over the coals.

Here is a story of how a physician tried to provide services for those who couldn't afford insurance by asking potential patients for a "retainer" and co-payment for a specific treatment. He, it appears, was able to provide medical services for 1/10th of the cost as compared to the traditional method of going through the whole insurance process. For attorneys it is fairly common to be on retainers. That is OK. It doesn't hurt the insurance companies. When a doctor tries to emulate that approach to provide medical services, the State Insurance Department of the physician's location, pushed by the insurance industry, comes down on the doctor for providing a service only the insurance companies are qualified to **properly price**. Apparently they contend the doctor is not qualified to price his service as he sees fit. Plumbers beware, one of these days the insurance companies will invade your territory and they will be the only ones who will be qualified to price your services.

This particular physician apparently determined he can make a good profit providing medical services in his office based on a retainer and a co-payment. He doesn't have to deal with all the paperwork and bureaucratic nightmares. Insurance companies, and the politicians supporting them, will fight those enterprising physicians with all their might. Can you imagine what would happen if the citizens of this country were to learn that much better health care services could be provided for 1/10th of what we currently pay? Would we not silence that sucking sound of the money flying out of your pocket into the coffers of the insurance industry and your hardworking politicians? What a nightmare!

Now let me give you an example what impact insurance companies have on the charge for an MRI. If you, as a patient, don't want to deal with an insurance company and you want to pay cash for an MRI, you can reduce the cost by as much as 75%. The probability is that you think, who cares, as long as I don't have to pay the 25%. Well the insurance companies hope you feel this way. Since they may have a published co-payment of 20%, why should you even contemplate paying cash at a cost of 5% more? How silly! Well that is true. Even with the 75% reduction, your cost will still be higher for the MRI, but that is a small price to pay for your privacy and keeps information away from insurance companies. The more they know about your health, the costlier it is to you over time. That is a fact!

Since my wife has a catheter in her bladder, I must irrigate it on a regular schedule. For this purpose I am using a "0.9% Sodium Chloride Irrigation Solution." The solution has less saline than ocean water. Ocean water, on average, has a salinity of 3.5%. This salt water solution can only be obtained with a prescription. Why? What is the logic? What happened to "gargle with salt water?"

When her physician prescribed it through her regular pharmacy, the cost was $50.55. This was the co- payment, in essence $10.11 per 1000ml. Again, this was the co-payment which means the insurance company is covering the balance, right? Well, I found the same "0.9% Sodium Chloride Irrigation Solution" through an established medical supplier on the internet, not in Canada but in the good old USA, for $2.77 per 1000ml and that was the total price, not some co-payment. How in the world can the insurance company contend that they are saving the patient money, they actually make a profit on the co-payment in excess of $35 for these 5 bottles. I just had to share this information with you in case you are happy with your insurance carrier because they "ONLY" require you to pay a SMALL co- payment. President Reagan, once referring to the former Soviet Union, said "Trust, but Verify!"

RULES–RULES and more RULES

While some students graduate from high school and make a command decision to become a doctor and enter the college or university of their choice, some of their friends select another profession – Legal Services! The legal profession also has a major impact on the medical profession.

There is no question that there is always a minority in any group who will always feel they have been wronged and some actually have been. This then creates rules and laws which are primarily designed to punish carelessness and negligence but as a result true accidental errors are handled in the same fashion. As a result, all of us, the majority are impacted by idiotic rules. The insurance industry doesn't miss a trick to enrich themselves at your expense and came up with coverage for the medical profession called "Malpractice Insurance." Many physicians have to buy into this sham purely out of self- protection. **You, the patient, is paying for it!** Some very good, highly confident and super competent physicians have decided to announce up front to their patients that they don't carry malpractice insurance. They actually have reduced the charges to their patients if you will deal with them directly and by-pass the insurance companies.

Our health care system is a disaster. For the last 13 years, Medicare payments to the physicians have not kept pace with the increased medical costs. They have been cut and there is constant talk about further cutting the reimbursement rate to the physicians. If these cuts continue, the inevitable will result. Physicians will be forced to drop Medicare beneficiaries. The alleged reason for this is the noble endeavor of balancing the federal budget (stop laughing). Maybe they want to allocate enough money so that we can finance the unending pork-barrel spending, like the bridge to nowhere or destroy the infrastructure of foreign countries and then rebuild it with our tax dollars rather than spend the money for improving our country. Have you ever heard that the health care costs of senators and congresspersons have been severally impacted by our endless budget deficits? You are paying for their super de luxe healthcare while you try to find enough money in your personal budget to pay for your own. Fortunately, at least right now, you have a choice regarding your own health insurance, you don't have to pay for it. For your favorite legislators you are not given that choice, you have to pay. I would call that a cozy arrangement for our "hardworking" legislators.

It is hard to say anything good about insurance companies. In dealing with them over a period of 45 years, I have no recollection of ever having heard – WOW, that was a good deed! This is the only industry falling into that category. If your criterion for a good and reliable insurance carrier is based on the fact that you get your premium notice 2 months ahead of schedule and they promptly cash your check, wait until you really need them and then publicize your endorsement.

Like I said in the beginning of this chapter…it's hard to write without anger.

Relationship with Medical Professionals

As a Caregiver your relationship with the medical profession will be just as important (and often more important) as the patient's. You must be aware of all the nuances, learn to clearly understand and not be shy to question any statement if you are not 100% certain of the meaning. A patient might accept things more readily when advised by "the professional." While the analysis, diagnosis or recommendation may possibly be correct, you, the caregiver needs to agree or articulate further questions to clarify issues. When both of you leave the office of "the professional" the patient will now be in your hands.

Let's now analyze how both of you fare as a caregiver/patient combination in the doctor's office. You might as well be aware in advance.

You make your appointment. You show up for your appointment a few minutes before the scheduled time. You sign in. They usually want to know what time you arrived and the time of your appointment. It's a memory test, to see if your memory is better than theirs.

You then sit down and wait to be called. While waiting you read all the signs and all the out-of-date magazines. I did find a sign saying that if you didn't cancel your appointment at least 24 hours before, you will be charged. Being extremely curious, I always search for the sign that tells me how much of a credit I get for every 15 minutes we don't get called in. I haven't found that sign but I keep on searching. In the early years of my retirement I did management consulting work, therefore time wasted represented a significant loss of income. One of the first doctors we made an appointment with in our new hometown had us waiting repeatedly in excess of 45 minutes. After several visits to this office, always with the same results, I approached the front desk. While waiting to be noticed, I looked at the sign-in log and realized that 3 people before us had the same appointment time, like 10:00AM, and then at 10:15AM we were scheduled with 2 other persons for the same time. In essence this office apparently scheduled at 5 minute intervals for each patient. When the front desk lady came up to the window, I asked her how much longer we would have to wait and I received a flip answer. That afternoon I sent a bill for my time to the physician. At the next appointment the physician and I had a very lively debate regarding his abusive time management practices. I don't know if my conversation with him ever changed his approach with patients because I gave him a credit, we walked out and never saw him again. This happened to be a unique experience and all the physicians we have been dealing with since then never practiced such disrespectful time management with their patients. There was only one occasion after our sour experience, when a doctor had been called to the hospital for an emergency and the staff properly informed the people in the waiting room. While waiting to be called, I usually find one of the most interesting articles in an old Reader's Digest magazine and before I can finish the intriguing story, we are being called in. The waiting game changes from the waiting room to the examination room. At least it gives you the impression of progress as patients disappear behind the entrance to the examination room area. Pretty soon a staff member shows up to check your temperature and pulse, take your blood pressure and go through the routine of listing all the medication you gave them the last time to make sure that the records are still accurate. Then comes the analytical question – why are you here today? These staff members run the gamut from extremely professional to thoroughly incompetent. Is this a cynical remark? Not at all! Here is a quote from one of the physicians. "I wish I could hire you, because you are a better nurse than the ones I have to deal with every day!"

Let's concentrate on the incompetent ones. You really don't know if they are incompetent when you meet them the first time. All I know is that I have never seen them before. I usually ask them if they are new to the profession or how long they have been in the broad category of the "health care environment," especially if they are drawing blood in order to avoid the "Oh, I am sorry!" remark.

If the answer is, "I just started this morning or something close to that," I start to worry. Why? I will give you an example which resulted in the dispensing of the wrong prescription. One of these newcomers to the medical profession made a mistake when she entered the dosage of a particular medication into the medical chart and several months later, when the pharmacy called for a prescription renewal, read the wrong dosage in. Because I pay attention to all medications when I pick them up, I noticed the error and called the doctor's office. First I had to go through the receptionist to leave a message for the person who called the medication in to the pharmacy. Eventually I received the return call. The attitude of the "medical professional" was plain and simple, "You are wrong, I called in the correct dosage!" That statement tickled my brain into action and I couldn't help it when I responded, "Like hell I am!" Look at the chart again, and look at an entry made six months ago. A somewhat testy dialog ensued and the "medical professional" finally admitted that in searching through the chart, several months back the wrong dosage was entered into the chart. How was I able to pinpoint the time? Six months ago I took my wife for an appointment and I remember having a feeling of utter dismay when the "professional" took my list of medications and kept on asking questions to which the answers were clearly spelled out on the sheet I had handed to her. The lady finally apologized and I received a valued commendation when she said, "Sir, wow – you are very observant."

Caregivers – be aware at all times – it is part of your job.

After the person leaves the examination room and places your folder into the holder outside by the door, you prepare yourself for the doctor's arrival. In your mind you rehearse the description of the patient's problems. Remember, your language doesn't necessarily match the medical expressions and the doctor has to translate your description into something meaningful to him or her. Make sure the physician understood what you said, don't assume the physician is as knowledgeable about you as you are about yourself, after all they have many patients with potentially similar conditions.

Has it ever crossed your mind that the physician may not have a clue what the problem is? Do you doubt this statement? Don't! I have been in an emergency room for ten hours, undergoing test after test and no conclusion was reached because they missed the obvious. That is the nature of the beast. Don't ever be afraid to ask questions, It is your health, your body and your well being that is at stake. Don't ever be silenced by condescending looks! While "the professional" may view you as an amateur, keep one thing in mind, an amateur built the ark, professionals built the Titanic!

Many times it may be a hit and miss encounter, no different than everything you do in your life. You have to understand that physicians are human beings, just like you and I, with the same frailties we are all endowed with. The key is, you are responsible for your own body or, if you are a caregiver, for the loved one you are keeping afloat. There is no satisfaction in being able to say that whoever treated you was "dead wrong," because the probability is very high that the physician may have been "wrong" but you or your loved one is "dead."

An important question! Are you satisfied with the performance of your physician(s)? Here are some important value points.

- When you call your doctor's office, do you get a return call in a reasonable time?
- Can you get an appointment when you have an urgent requirement and I mean truly urgent or are you referred to the emergency room? Physicians should be able to accommodate your request that same day or at least the following day. When you get an answer like, "The next open time is five weeks from now," look for a different doctor now, this is not the one you want to have to deal with when you really need help.
- In the rare case when you need to talk to your doctor after hours or on weekends, what is the response? Does he or she answer the page of the answering service in a reasonably short time? When you talk to the physician do you get the cop-out answer, i.e. "go to the emergency room" or do you actually get a rational response or suggestion? Obviously, in today's litigiously crazy society, the physician must be careful how to answer your question. If you have been his or her patient for more than 10 years and you always maintained a cordial relationship, you should not get the cop-out answer. If yes, find yourself a different physician because he or she really doesn't give a damn.

- How does the office staff treat you? You should never be inhibited. Speak up if you feel you are not being treated fairly or with respect. They are there to help you. You are the patient, the "buyer" of their service.
- Once you have entered the examination room, watch out for a few things such as; what is the balance of "Nurse Time" to "Doctor Time?" You came to see the doctor, not the nurse. When the doctor enters the room, ask yourself these questions: Does he or she actually know who you are? Do you feel like you are being treated as a new patient? Does he or she actually listen to you? Is he or she dismissive? Does he or she have to review the chart excessively? Is he or she a pill pusher (recommending new medications to replace older and effective ones)? Don't make the assumption that the doctor is up-to-date about your situation or condition, he or she has many patients, some with similar complaints. If you think he or she has forgotten something or doesn't seem to pay attention, speak up. If all the above mentioned negatives pile up, look for a different doctor.
- Make sure your test results are available for inspection or try to get a copy. You may not understand all the hieroglyphics but at least you can compare previous readings to current ones. Blood tests usually show desirable ranges and if you are within those ranges or not.
- How does your doctor feel about second opinions? Does he or she encourage them or do you get the feeling that he or she resents such a proposal? Keep in mind that as a caregiver you can be viewed by your physician as a "second opinion." Some doctors actually get jealous when you "the neophyte" enter the inner sanctum of the studied profession. The fact that as a caregiver you are an expert regarding one and only one patient doesn't enter their mind. This observation is based on real life experiences.

Finally, while the relationship with your physician(s) is extremely important – don't ever forget the VALUE of the relationship with the office staff. They may not be responsible for saving a person's life, but they are definitely responsible for saving your sanity!

Standard Pain,
Hunger Pain and Nerve Pain.

There is a big difference between STANDARD PAIN, HUNGER PAIN and NERVE PAIN. We are quite familiar with what most of us refer to as PAIN. We get a paper cut, it is painful. We hit our toes against the table leg, we know it. You walk and suddenly trip, you may twist your ankle; you have a PAIN. This PAIN is transmitted by the nerves to the brain and you are acutely aware of it. Most of these PAINS respond to over-the-counter medications or some sort of therapy including massaging.

NERVE PAIN originates in the central nervous system. Multiple Sclerosis (MS) not only attacks the myelin or the insulating material of the nerves, but nerve pathways are also damaged, causing these nerve pains or neuropathic events. MS is not the only disease which can produce nerve pain.

Nerve pain can happen very suddenly and can manifest itself in a variety of ways, like an electrical shock. The patient may even experience a pain in a limb which, otherwise, actually has no feeling. Sometimes the patient may suddenly complain about the weight of the comforter covering the body. A person not afflicted by these symptoms can be perplexed because it is quite difficult to comprehend. Obviously we experience pain from our point of view and just assume that we all feel pain in the same way and that the weight of the comforter can't possibly be painful.

To complicate matters, there also is HUNGER PAIN. A healthy person is aware when you have a feeling of being hungry. It is not a very thought provoking exercise to identify it or even waste much time before you hit the refrigerator in search of the cure.

For a person afflicted by any disease or affliction, it can get difficult to distinguish this pain for those induced by other reasons. In this case, the caregiver's power of observation may contribute to the identification of this pain. For example, was the patient influenced by one of the many highly enticing TV food or restaurant commercials which show delicious entrees in a beautiful setting and color? These commercials are obviously intended to have that impact on your mind, including the disabled. Your power of observation becomes very important!

In addition, it is very important that the caregiver encourages the patient to be specific in describing the pain, like stabbing, electrical shock like feeling plus the location and frequency of the attacks. I feel sick or I have a pain will not do! If food or normal pain medication doesn't seem to work, then one has to try an anti-convulsing drug. There are a number of drugs available and believe it or not, it is a trial and error type process to determine which of these drugs the patient responds to best.

It is not uncommon for patients to wait for months before they finally consult their physician. Many patients feel, why should I complain, my disease, in our case MS, is just getting worse. NERVE PAIN can be brought under control, DO NOT IGNORE IT!

It took quite a while before my wife and I clearly identified this particular PAIN. She would complain about her left leg which basically has no feeling. She had a sledding accident many years ago which damaged her leg and caused severe pain. Originally we were perplexed that these pains would re-occur and tried to treat them with a strong pain medication. It showed no immediate result but over time it became more subdued and we were fooled into believing that the medication was doing the trick. Then we had an experience when she had a pain on the left side of her face. The first thought, why does this always happen on the left side? This was harder to eliminate and we finally reached the conclusion that this was tooth related. So we went to the dentist. The dentist took an X-ray and poked around, but couldn't find anything. What was most perplexing was the fact that my wife complained about pain in one tooth that didn't have a nerve because of root canal work and a false tooth. In the evolutionary description under **YEAR 39** this whole episode is clearly explained. A re-occurrence ten years later is covered under **YEAR 49** when the dental expert we saw at that time recommended to have all the teeth pulled and replaced with a new set of dentures. My question: How do we know that it will eliminate the pain if she has pain in a tooth that doesn't have a nerve and none of the nerves close to that tooth show an infection or other problem? His response killed me. He said if she still has pain after all the teeth have been removed, we know for sure it is caused by something else. I told him, I think that is a draconian step to take to solve a non-existing problem. I thanked him for his attempt to get his old BMW replaced with a newer version at my expense. As explained before, in the meantime we had already found the solution through her Neurologist who recommended an increase of her Neurontin for a short time.

The episode in **YEAR 39** was solved with a cream containing Neurontin. At that time the Neurologist explained that Neurontin has had a favorable impact on some MS patients, why was not clear, so he prescribed it for use whenever she had an attack. He explained that the dosage could be increased considerably during an attack but in general she should be maintained on a maintenance dosage. Now my wife has infrequent attacks but in treating it with Neurontin and some other medication which has been added, the nerve pain can be brought under control within 15 to 20 minutes. It took a while to find out what the problem was, but now it has made her life at little more livable.

NERVE PAIN manifests itself in weird ways. The patient will benefit tremendously if the caregiver is observant and can diagnose the problem expeditiously.

Medication and Food
(The Good, the Bad and the Ugly)

Are we better off today than our forefathers? The answer is YES and NO.

Our parents smoked cigarettes, cigars and chewed tobacco. We know or at least have been informed, that the manufacturers of tobacco products knowingly have caused cancer to humans and have really been made to pay for misleading us. They really didn't stick the cigarettes into your mouth but who cares, they were evil.

The oil companies get away with poisoning our environment because we rather die than walk. Smoking cigarettes may cause cancer, but inhaling the exhaust fumes from our cars (carbon monoxide) can kill you faster than cancer.

Drinking alcoholic beverages, while widespread, hasn't been blamed for any particular disease causing event. The fact that the brain suffers and deteriorates isn't really enough to go after the producers of alcoholic beverages. If someone gets caught driving while under the influence, at least lets fine them heavily, maybe take their driver's license away so that they can't earn a living and pay the next fine for driving illegally, even if not intoxicated. We fixed their wagon the smart way, right? We punish the producers of alcoholic beverages by taking away their privilege to advertise on TV.

FDA approved drugs seem to kill more people than illegal drugs, but their advertising privileges have not been inhibited. They are allowed to mislead us, after all they have more resources to pay your elected officials than the tobacco manufacturers had. As long as they warn the public of all the bad things that could possibly happen to you, using minuscule small print and hieroglyphics, they are off the hook. Now the problem has been transferred from them to you or maybe your doctor. So let us talk about this life threatening issue which I will call *Pharmaceutical propaganda!*

After reading this, your reaction may be, "But we are doing better and don't we live longer?" How would you know that we are better off? Has the constant drumbeat and propaganda made you numb and you are repeating what you hear? The pharmaceutical industry has an ongoing campaign to convince you that if it wasn't for all their good pills, you would be as bad off as the generation that preceded you. Here's the question I want for you to ponder, have they made things better or worse? Their propaganda is endless and totally misleading. The latest report available lists the 4th leading cause of death in the US are FDA approved drugs, a number exceeding 100,000 per year.

Let's compare that to war death:

American Civil War:	154,000 per war year
World War II:	125,000 per war year
Korean War:	20,000 per war year
Vietnam War:	5,800 per war year
Iraq War (estimate):	760 per war year

The major improvements have to be attributed to the medical profession, their techniques and the equipment to support them. Pharmaceutical companies played a role, like the development of penicillin, but in comparison to the medical profession, it is no way as dramatic an improvement.

It is no secret that pharmaceutical companies are very powerful commercial enterprises. They allocate a huge amount to advertising in order to let you know how they have an answer to a disease and if that isn't enough, they will invent another "syndrome" for which they can market another pill. Their whole intent is to fill their coffers with tons of money, your money extracted from your purse or hip pocket by telling you to ask your doctor if whatever they are pushing will help an affliction that you didn't know you had, or that even existed, until you saw the TV commercial. That's why they worked so hard to convince your congress to deny you the opportunity to buy their brand name medication from a foreign country for half the price. They are so concerned about your well being, they want to protect you from all these potential "counterfeit meds" in their original packaging. In my foreign travels, I have bought refills in foreign countries, the exact same medication as the one I purchased in a local pharmacy before my trip. It was 50% less. The irony, all these foreign countries allegedly must be using potentially fake medication and it doesn't change anything; maybe it only proves that the original medication really doesn't help either.

When they list the potential side effects, one cannot help but wonder, what is worse, the affliction or the consequences of using the medication. *Have you ever read the SIDE EFFECTS of a medication?* Following is the side effect language of a common and widely used medication. It has been on the market for over six years. I encourage you to read it carefully. Any comedian could easily develop a hilarious one hour comedy routine using this material.

> POSSIBLE SIDE EFFECTS: Side Effects that may occur while taking this medicine include diarrhea, gas, headache, indigestion, nausea, stomach upset, temporary metallic taste, or vomiting. If they continue or are bothersome, check with your doctor. CONTACT YOUR DOCTOR IMMEDIATELY if you experience chest pain or discomfort; dizziness or lightheadedness, fast or difficult breathing, fever, chills, or persistent sore throat; feeling of being unusually cold, general feeling of being unwell; muscle pain or weakness, slow or irregular heartbeat; unusual or persistent stomach pain or discomfort; unusual drowsiness; unusual tiredness or weakness. Allergic reaction to this medicine is unlikely, but seek immediate medical attention if it occurs. Symptoms of an allergic reaction include rash, itching, swelling, severe dizziness, or trouble breathing. If you notice other effects not listed above, contact your doctor, nurse or pharmacist. This is not a complete list of all the side effects that may occur. (Is this possible? I can't possibly think of anything else that could go wrong!) If you have questions about side effects, contact your healthcare provider. Call your doctor for medical advice about side effects. You may report side effects to the FDA at 1-800-FDA-1088.

(FDA stands for Food & Drug Administration). Coincidently 1-800-DEA-1088 (DEA stands for Drug Enforcement Administration). Is it answered by the same people??? Was the number 1-800-332-1088 used in order to create either acronym? Coincidence or on purpose?

If the drug companies can list so many potential side effects, are they not making a clear statement that each human being will react differently to their medication? Shouldn't it then be equally clear that the beneficial aspects they so freely promote may be just as questionable?

What do you think of this one and I quote, "If you have diarrhea or are vomiting and it is bothersome, check with your doctor." Is it customary to have a telephone in each bathroom and by the kitchen sink?

At no time are you asked to call the manufacturer of the medication. They don't give a warranty for their products. Imagine if you were to buy a car from your favorite manufacturer and you would get a list of potential problems, such as your brakes may fail. When it happens, you may feel anxiety or sheer panic as you approach a cliff, or if you jump out of the car and hit a tree, you may end up with a king size headache, or suddenly have diarrhea or start vomiting and if you are **bothered** by these side effects, call your mechanic immediately.

Some time ago I complained several times to my doctor about side effects regarding chest pains and potential heart problems when I was using two different medications he had prescribed. His response was for me to enlist in the army and seek an assignment in my favorite war zone. He said, "This way, if you die, you will be a war hero and may even be buried at Arlington Cemetery." In essence, GET OFF MY BACK!

In their commercials you are never encouraged to check all these wonder drugs with your pharmacist. After all, those are the individuals who know the medication better than the doctor. Why is the doctor the focus of their commercials? They can prescribe the medication not the pharmacist.

I find it strange that physicians have not rebelled against the pharmaceutical companies, who in their TV ads encourage their male patients to call their doctor immediately when something doesn't happen. Why burden your doctor who probably had nothing to do with the undesirable situation. Why should he or she be responsible? I am referring to the erectile dysfunction medications. Why don't the pharmaceutical companies have their own staff on duty to answer calls? They are the ones making a fortune promoting those pills. The chances that these problems are encountered during day light hours are probably less. It would be my guess that if there is a problem, it would be sometime during the evening hours. If you were a doctor, what would you do? I asked our doctor and he had a fabulous answer. I am not sure the patients would be receptive to his solution.

If you were in business selling whatever product and it was a high income producer, would you really want this product to wipe out the market, in essence would it be smart business to totally cure a disease? No way! Portraying something that will "improve" your condition not cure it, while at the same time trying to convince you that they will leave no stone unturned in their effort to search for the ultimate cure, is a much better income producing strategy. With the alleged progress, shouldn't we see an increase in the elimination of diseases not an increase of new and ever growing "syndromes?"

The pharmaceutical industry is quite successful in their effort to create the "forever" income stream if possible. One example is a combo. This combination is perfect, who doesn't want to keep the blood pressure under control and at the same time reduce the cholesterol. Can't beat that! Just ask your doctor, is he or she really going to turn you down by saying, "Hey, just run around the block six times a day and you will normalize your blood pressure and feel good. While you are running around, take a bag of carrots along and you will see your cholesterol dropping."

The human body is a "Wonder Machine." It is a fairly tolerant entity. From early on in our lives, we abuse this "Wonder Machine" with no overt consequences as a result of our neglect or carelessness.

At some point along the path from birth to the end of our life cycle we will encounter problems very much related to our treatment of this wonder machine. In the majority of the cases, unfortunately not all, we then have an opportunity to seek the advice of a professional, usually the family doctor, who we see as the expert in the complexity of the human body. Does any human being really understand the complexities? The fact is that there are many specialties in the medical field which clearly demonstrates the diversity of the human body. Even within these specialties, test results and observations can produce significantly different interpretations.

This analysis can be summarized into one sentence. "Change your life-style; it will change your destiny!"

The human body needs hundreds of minerals to be properly balanced in order to continue as a life supporting "Wonder Machine." Shortages, lack thereof or excesses of substances have an impact on the fine tuned performance of the human body. It is not a robotic machine produced from a technically defined blueprint, but is a unique and individualized entity. How do we make sure the body is getting its proper dosage and what is the proper dosage. Blood tests will provide some partial insight. The general description of life-style changes concentrates mostly on the consumption of total fat, saturated fat, trans fat, cholesterol, sodium, illegal drugs, excessive alcohol and the effect of smoking to your health.

This is not a guide of what your nutrition should be, it is only intended to motivate you to make progress by setting goals and celebrating the achievement of each step to further motivate you forward.

We are familiar with some of the most common substances which have an impact on the proper performance of the human body, like vitamins and nutritional elements supplemented by FDA approved medications.

After this introduction of the general workings of the "Wonder Machine" let's direct our attention to the pharmaceutical industry.

Much can be said about pharmaceutical companies and their role in our lives or better yet, their efforts to produce medications which hopefully will extend the life of patients in need.

Over time these companies have become powerhouses and exercise tremendous influence in how they serve their stockholders. Among them they are fiercely competitive and as such attempt to hit the market with a blockbuster pill if at all possible, the blue pill Viagra was such a hit. Since the introduction of Viagra, a number of different names have been introduced competing with the initial entry. Some of these are portrayed as "better."

THE GOOD

This industry, without a doubt, has contributed tremendously to the well being of humans and animals alike through the discovery or development of medication suited to relieve pain and suffering for millions. As I said before, one major entry was Penicillin, which during World War II reduced, the number of death as a result of infected wounds by more than 10% amongst our troops.

Fortunately, the medical profession also made great strides using new techniques and with the use of advanced equipment are able to perform fabulous life saving procedures. As an example, since the Civil War in the 1860's to now, war deaths per war year have steadily declined during each successive war to only one half of a percent of those that died during the Civil War. The vast majority of these survival statistics are a result of the combination of the medical profession and the dedicated research by pharmaceutical companies.

Why does all this really matter to you if you are not a happy investor but a caregiver or patient? Excessive power by those who have a direct impact on your life and wellbeing can also adversely influence your decisions when it comes to issues of life and death A healthy person probably will not lose to much sleep regarding medication announcements or commercials and what these drugs correct, the disease they may relieve or whatever new "syndrome" they attack, except in an abstract way. For them it's like worrying about brands of gas for their car, if the price is right and the car doesn't cough, do they really care?

The patient or caregiver must be as informed as possible. An uninformed decision can have life threatening consequences and ironically, your interests aren't necessarily on the same frequencies as those of the pharmaceutical companies.

They have stockholders who want to see them making a good profit so they can receive their earned reward, the dividend, but this effort by the pharmaceutical industry doesn't necessarily translate into a benefit to you or your patient.

THE BAD

Example 1: The lobbying effort by the industry to make sure their identical products sold to foreign countries for a lower price cannot be re-introduced into the US at that reduced price, i.e. legal drugs from

Canada. Obviously this is only intended to increase their profits at your expense. When I say your expense, it doesn't matter if it is paid by your insurance or not, in the end you are paying for it through higher insurance premiums. The industry will rationalize it in the most heart warming expressions to demonstrate that they only have your continued good health at heart by protecting you from counterfeit medication.

Example 2: In the not too distant past, a study was published that 81 mg of Aspirin had a favorable impact by potentially preventing a heart attack. The pharmaceutical industry ran with that one, they introduced the 81 mg Aspirin. They reduced it from 325 mg, a 75% reduction in size (less aspirin) which was the common version before this major discovery and now offered this new wonder pill at a price 11% higher than the 325mg version.

Example 3: A pain medication commercial asks you to tell your doctor if you have a kidney or liver problem. Until I heard this commercial I was under the misguided impression that it was the doctor who would give me the bad news.

The physician is your paid professional consultant who is expected to diagnose your malady and then prescribe a remedy, including the appropriate medication, which hopefully will put you on your path toward recovery. After your visit, you may ask your pharmacist, "the medication specialist," for an opinion about the interaction between your prescribed and non-prescribed medication and if there is a better, more cost effective alternative available.

In the end, these are the people you will have to work with constantly, not the pharmaceutical companies.

Let me repeat what I said before. Ask yourself a simple question. Why do pharmaceutical companies encourage you to discuss all their offerings with your doctor rather than "the pharmaceutical product expert," the pharmacist? The doctor writes the prescription, not the pharmacist.

Example 4: The promotion of "combo drugs." One such expensive combo drug is supposed to lower your blood pressure and cholesterol. The TV commercial promoting this medication is intended to convince you that it has to be good. What a winner, one pill attacking two major concerns in one shot, what a bargain. Is it really?

It is amazing how our population always responds to anything that allegedly provides instant results. WOW! One pill which attacks the two ills we hear so much about and at the same time. A combo drug should only be considered if the cost is less or at least equivalent to the combination of the individual drugs. Let's take a look at these two prescription drugs. The one intended to lower blood pressure is best taken in the morning. The other one, intended to lower cholesterol, works best when taken before going to bed. The body supposedly produces more cholesterol at night. Isn't there an obvious conflict? In addition, one of the stated side effects of this type of a drug is the possibility of muscle inflammation, something your heart wouldn't condone. That "meaningless little conflict" is resolved by the pharmaceutical propaganda machine encouraging you (the patient) to call your doctor and tell him what your ailments are before he prescribes this medication to you. As I said before, I find this approach very strange. I was brought up to believe that it was the doctor who would tell me what medical problems I had, not the other way around. When did this change?

Example 5: Some MS patients have what is referred to as remissions. In a different chapter of this book I describe remissions. The pharmaceutical industry decided to develop medication to extend remissions. Who wouldn't want to forget about MS and push it further away? There is one problem. Remissions can last a short time or a long time, there is really no scientific rule, therefore when one takes the medication to extend the remission, you can't measure it against anything. I have documented my wife's progression and found remissions of multiple lengths and she has taken no medication. I have talked to other MS patients who spend a ton of money on these medications and they are convinced what the industry told them is correct and therefore it is worth the expenditure. The truth is, one can give a placebo to a MS patient and tell them the remission will be extended and some will swear it definitely is. The pharmaceutical industry sides with the believers; for them the believers are, without a doubt, more profitable than the non-believers. Most medications for MS exclude those with "Progressive MS." Those are the most severely afflicted who do not experience remissions. They are generally on a steady downhill slope. This then raises a question in my mind. How does the medication know that a particular patient has progressive MS rather then the "remission" version? I then wonder, is it possible that the pill really doesn't have a clue, but the pharmaceutical companies know that it is much easier to convince the "remission" MS people that whatever may conceivably happen naturally is actually being helped through these pills, even if the pill isn't responsible for it. The progressive patient, who wouldn't see any benefit, would have a hard time buying this propaganda.

Why the pharmaceutical industry hasn't combined a drug to help overcome constipation with the other drug which does just the opposite, is a mystery to me. Can you image taking one pill per day for the rest of your life and never again being in a panic when in search for an unlocked bathroom? This would be the ultimate blockbuster pill. I think the pharmaceutical companies could take credit for extending the life of all takers because it would lower the stress level forever. Every person taking these pills would never again have to face either of these undesirable conditions, but then, "What do I know, I am only a cynic!"

THE UGLY

There is one troubling fact. The latest report available lists as the 4th leading cause of death in the US, FDA approved drugs, a number exceeding 100 thousand per year. A more specific example is the fact that of FDA approved drugs during the last quarter century, 20% had severe side effects not known when approved. That is 1 in 5!

The flashy TV advertising campaign by this industry is partially responsible for this. Without going into details, you, the afflicted party, is encouraged to ask your physician for whatever medication is being promoted. Invariably it lists all the potential side effects at a mind numbing speed or on the bottom of your TV screen with the same small letters the "Used Car sales people" promote their fabulous offers. Surprisingly, alcohol and tobacco (cigarettes) commercials are banned from TV. Shouldn't the 4th leading cause of death, FDA approved drugs, also be banned from TV? Wouldn't a ban potentially reduce medication costs because they would have to compete with results not propaganda?

The amount of FDA approved TV drug advertising far exceeds that of any other major category and it is constant. How much do you think this TV advertising campaign really adds to the cost of your prescription?

A bundle! Mind you, it still has to be prescribed; you can't just go to the pharmacy and request it. You still have to pay your doctor, who I view as a consultant, and tell him or her which medical maladies you have before they can prescribe the medication. Hopefully this little conversation with the doctor will diminish the possibility of side effects. This is the only relationship where the consultant (doctor) gets paid to listen to you instead of the other way around. Wouldn't you like to have such a job? The drug manufacturers seem to have figured out that it is much easier to sell their merchandise to the general public, the suckers, than to the professionals who are less gullible.

The sign of a caring doctor is the one who refuses to just go along with your request as a result of your being influenced by one of these drug company's TV commercials. A good doctor will take a few minutes out of his busy schedule and explain to you why it may be wiser to take a less costly alternative or no drug at all. A good example is the old fashioned diuretic or "water pill." Studies have shown that the old fashioned pills are just as effective as the new highly touted drugs performing basically the same function. For the price of the old fashioned pills you will have effective coverage for more than two months versus one day of the new and highly touted replacement. Obviously it is a ploy to transfer monies from your pocket into the coffers of the new drug providers.

We live in a world of sound bites, repetitive commercials, distorted and out of context statements and sometimes outright propaganda. Many of these pieces are at the very edge of illegality but are false portrayals nevertheless. Aggressive attorneys find ways to make cases against a number of issues because they are really at the border between real and false. Attorneys also advise their clients on how the law can be circumvented legally. This is pretty much true with any commercial enterprise. In regard to pharmaceutical companies and their products it is done by rattling off an endless stream of potential side effects, some of which seem to require a medical degree to even understand, and if that is the case, it certainly complicates understanding the potential interrelationship with other drugs. By doing this, now you have been notified, now it's your problem.

The drive for profits, a commendable attribute if you are a non disabled or healthy stockholder, may be in direct conflict with the requirements for the DISABLED stockholder. In this scenario, the disabled person is attracted to the pharmaceutical company's inventiveness with an eye toward the financial rewards this may create, but potential side effects of this "winner drug" could lead to his or her demise.

Awareness and attention to detail is extremely important. There is nothing wrong with questioning all statements and attempting to understand the motivation behind why statements are made. This is not limited to pharmaceutical companies and the products they promote, this is important for any caregiver. Ironically, in the end you will invariably be judged by your personal acts and when something happens which affects your patient or the loved one you are caring for, society unfortunately will judge you harshly no matter what "commercials" promised. It is your responsibility to do your utmost to protect your patient from any potential harm, therefore reading between the lines is a necessity.

Don't be gullible and believe all these flashy commercials.

Nutrition

Socrates said, "If you are sick turn to nutrition first before medication." I don't know if he said it, I wasn't visiting Greece at the time, but it is a wise expression and it makes a lot of sense.

From a caregiver's point of view, one of the major concerns or issues is the proper maintenance of the patient. Nutrition, what you eat and drink, is at the top of the list. Exercise, while important, may not be possible as a result of the severity of the disability, at least with the intensity necessary to make much of a difference. Medication will become a significant addition when nutrition alone, in a broad sense, cannot accomplish the task at hand.

The following is the definition of "Nutrition" in the Webster Dictionary. "Nutrition is the act or process by which organism, whether plant or animal is assimilated and converted from food to tissue." It is not just eating and drinking the "Right Stuff." A Caregiver or professional nutritionist must prepare a specifically tailored nutrition plan for the patient based on the needs and requirements of the person. The menus and generalized concepts promoted in TV commercials as well as in a large variety of books may be helpful, but there is a high probability that certain modifications must be made for the particular patient.

If you are not comfortable developing a proper nutrition plan, I urge you to see a nutritional expert or professional and while you are at it, get a plan for yourself, after all, you are supposed to outlast the patient.

This book is intended to give a caregiver some ideas what he or she may face and how to deal with it. It is not a cookbook. In order to make a point, I will describe a learning experience, a sequence of events which caused my wife (the patient) to almost perish as a result of mal-nutrition. The deleterious progress went unnoticed by all parties involved until the body suddenly decided to shut down.

My wife was encountering a problem with the catheters; in essence they had to be changed more frequently than would be deemed normal. During this whole period, she was given properly balanced and nutritious food. She had problems utilizing the utensils and as a result left more food unfinished. The answer by the therapist was to attach a strap around her wrist. This strap was designed to assure that the spoon or fork wouldn't fall out of her hand, in essence, keep the frustration level to a bare minimum. While focusing on correcting the food input, an infection was building up in the kidney and the patient's appetite appeared to diminish. The strap didn't accomplish much and I resorted to spoon feeding my wife. In spite of this change, my wife still wasn't eating more because unbeknownst to her, swallowing ever so slowly became an increased problem. So here, the proper food was being fed, most of it mashed to simplify the swallowing process, but in spite of it, my wife was still going down-hill. This particular experience shows that malnutrition can be caused by other not so obvious reasons. In this case, the impact of the slow progression of an unobserved infection coupled with diminished intake of the proper and balanced food arrived at the same time and became a life threatening emergency.

This was the low point. After being treated for all the problems which caused the emergency, the issue of nutrition had to be addressed, since my wife still had not changed her eating habits. It was then that the professionals uncovered that the reaction time of the epiglottis, the medical term for what I refer to as the little traffic cop in our throat which closes access to the lungs when you are eating and flips back when you have to inhale, had slowed down.

A perfectly healthy person probably will never think about the process that takes place when you bite into an apple, chew it and then swallow while at the same time being able to talk without choking. It is that little traffic cop in our throat which makes sure air goes to and from the lungs while the food ends up in your stomach and not in your lungs.

This disabled person's "traffic director" was extremely lethargic and slow. It could not guarantee that the patient would not choke while eating or drinking.

A PEG tube (the medical expression for a feeding tube) had to be inserted into the stomach in order to feed my wife without fear of something taking to long on its trip to the stomach and causing the patient to choke. Since the feeding tube was inserted, the progress to a better functioning body has been extraordinary. Quite an accomplishment! The skin is healing faster and better, the fingernails were soft before, now they are hardened and like little sharp knives, the bodily functions are normal all because the nutritional supplements are well balanced and designed for this specific body. The caloric intake is calculated in order to maintain a desired weight. A totally disabled person doesn't have the luxury of running a few miles on a treadmill, so careful weight maintenance is very critical. In order to exercise the throat muscles, it is important to still feed the patient easy to swallow food items such as apple sauce, mashed potatoes and those delicacies which truly melt in your mouth. Any roughage such as cereals, nuts, chips and other such items are not desirable and should be discouraged.

Somehow people are under the impression that if you have a feeding tube in your belly, you are in bad shape. It isn't necessarily true. This little "head scratching" exchange between my wife and me shows that. A healthy person doesn't have the same option as the one with a feeding tube in her stomach. I had to administer some medication to my wife and asked her, "Please, open your mouth, I have to give you a spoonful of your medication!" Her response was, "That medication tastes horrible, administer it through the feeding tube, but you can give me some applesauce instead." I saw the logic of her request, but had to laugh.

All the medication is administered through the feeding tube. Medication that is not available in liquid form is crushed in a special pill crusher available at a medical supply store or some pharmacy and then dissolved in water before introducing it through the feeding tube.

As you can see, there is more to nutrition than meets the eye. It is an intricate process, not a hamburger and soda.

Again I need to stress VIGILANCE. Caregiving is an extremely interesting job. You can contribute to medical science by not only being a caregiver but a medical researcher. Many people would flock to the Caregiving profession if the pay would be a bit more than ZERO.

Looking at the human race from the broadest point of view, we are dealing with two major categories,

Losers and Winners.

Losers are those who are negative, have no imagination, retreat from any challenge, are stubborn, are jealous of winners and as a result will never excel. You will find them in the section called "Feelings." You can't be a caregiver if you are a "Loser."

Winners are those who are positive, have a "can do" attitude, are willing to learn from others, use other winners as their role models, never give up and want to excel at whatever they undertake. To be a caregiver, you must be a "Winner."

So here are some suggestions for the "Winner" caregiver. First and foremost you must understand that your medical research is one of specificity not based on generalities. Medical research is usually conducted with a large controlled group, one which takes the placebo and another group takes a specific medication, food or supplement. The results are averaged. Some of the placebo group may actually show improvements because of mind power.

The caregiver medical research is conducted with one person and only one, the patient. Careful documentation is absolutely mandatory. As an example I will share the conclusions we have reached as a result of our individualized research with this one disabled patient.

The summary point: Keep caloric intake low. It not only keeps weight down but less calories reduces free radicals; those are molecules which introduce biochemical damage. Eat more bulk in the form of fruits and vegetables, lower in calories but in general are nutritionally healthy and contain antioxidants to help immunize your body against the damaging free radicals.

The main component is the tube-fed nutritional supplement which is complemented by small individual servings of applesauce, garlic soup, a spoonful of honey, mashed avocados with olive oil, little bit of vinegar and onion powder or mildly seasoned mashed potatoes and water.

Applesauce: Why? Potentially prevents cancer and reduces constipation.

Avocadoes prepared as outlined: Why? The combination is an arteries protector, strong antioxidant, thins the blood, decreases the bad cholesterol (LDL) and increases the good cholesterol (HDL), fights diabetes by regulating blood sugar, high in potassium thus reducing leg cramps.

Garlic: Why? To reduce blood pressure, reduce cholesterol; help the immune system fight off potential afflictions. This patient has been healthy except for the underlying disease. The best way is to prepare a delicious garlic soup, twice a week, using fresh garlic and spinach plus other ingredients. With that much garlic one would assume that it would have a heavy garlic flavor, but in reality there isn't a hint of it. You can be assured that after consumption of this soup, your friends will still speak to you, face to face.

Garlic should be raw. Cooking will somewhat diminish its potency. Those that prefer the proverbial shortcut and take the odorless pill instead are giving up the clot-removing capability of fresh garlic. The pill bottle may have a statement something like this. "Garlic helps maintain cholesterol levels at a normal range." What is the normal range? They don't say, but one would assume that a reading of less than 200 is desirable.

One teaspoon of Honey: Why? It has antibiotic elements.

Mildly seasoned mashed potatoes and water, why? Since potatoes are high in potassium it will diminish the possibility of cramps and is somewhat helpful to keep blood pressure down.

Sufficient fresh water to provide proper hydration and to make sure that the urine is clear and mildly yellowish.

The above is just a synopsis of a number of conclusions we have reached as a result of our on-going research on the effects of the nutritional elements and the medication the patient is taking on a daily basis. This is then supplemented with the usual tests for blood pressure, temperature and glucose levels.

By carefully monitoring the patient, there were a number of cases where a visit to the emergency room was prevented.

There are a number of books published by Rodale, Bottom Line Books and Prevention Magazine Health Books which can be extremely helpful to a caregiver who really wants to become well versed in the Caregiving job. You have to be open-minded and understand that not all recommendations made are applicable to all people. Remember what I said before, human bodies are unique entities and not robotic creatures.

Hospital Patient Representative/Caregiver

When a patient, any patient, for whatever reason, has been admitted to the hospital, it is strongly recommended that a caregiver and/or family member be "on guard duty" with the patient, especially if the patient is a disabled person and admitted to ICU. As a caregiver and advocate for my wife I encountered a number of unfortunate experiences, one of which is worth detailing. Rarely did I find faults with the nursing staff. In general terms, they were excellent and attentive. Depending on their workload, which by design is limited to fewer patients in ICU as compared to the regular hospital rooms, attentiveness is a matter of perception. The individual patient suffering can't get attention fast enough and the nurses must weigh this against all the patients under their care. That is normal and in most instances is not the problem. It is the system which is flawed. Here is an example.

During an earlier stay at the ICU unit of a hospital, one of the family members on duty called me at 3AM to inform me that my wife had been given a morphine shot. I immediately went to the hospital to inquire why they felt compelled to administer morphine, especially since my wife had taken some potent painkillers before but it had never reached the level of morphine. The nurse explained that my wife was complaining about a severe pain so she called the doctor and he prescribed it. I wanted to know what particular severe pain my wife was complaining about and she responded, "Well, I really couldn't understand what she was saying and your family member also had great difficulties understanding her complaint." For your information, my wife sometimes has great difficulties formulating words and I have to resort to posing multiple specific questions with YES or NO answers or hand signals.

I went into the room and started to communicate with my wife in our own mode. It wasn't easy especially after the morphine shot which had not reduced the pain very much but was taking her on a trip into never-never land.

I was finally able to determine that she had a severe pain in her bladder region, which meant that there was something wrong with the catheter. I asked the nurse when they had replaced the catheter and was informed that the change occurred about two hours earlier. I inquired about the size and the amount of sterile solution used to inflate the balloon. To my utter amazement I realized that it was the wrong size catheter and they had over inflated the balloon. Instead of pushing the balloon into the bladder, it was inflated in the urethra which was causing the severe pain. I told the nurse to immediately remove it and place the correct one with the proper inflation. She said she couldn't do it unless the doctor ordered it and she didn't have the right size anyhow. I will not document my specific reaction other than that I told the nurse I will take full responsibility. I told her to remove the catheter immediately, which she did and guess what, the pain left with the catheter. I told her that I kept a number of the proper catheters at home. I wouldn't mind driving home and bringing one back. She said, "No, I can't use one of yours unless it is checked out by our people and they won't be in until the morning." One cannot argue with that precautionary position and I told her, I don't really care, find the right one later and in the meantime place sufficient absorbing material under her to keep her dry. Within an hour, they did find the right catheter and the situation was corrected.

The final comment by the nurse was most revealing.

"We have the RESPONIBILITY to take care of patients, we are held ACCOUNTABLE if anything goes wrong, but we do not have the AUTHORITY to do anything even if we have the correct answer to the problem based on our experience, unless approved by a doctor who may not respond as expeditiously as the situation may warrant."

The above description is a true example and I have experienced two other situations which potentially could have been fatal would I not have intervened. That is a flaw of the system! Occasionally we hear about "accidental" death in hospitals. Each year, approximately one hundred thousand patients succumb to various medical errors including wrong medication or dosage and it doesn't seem to warrant much attention. It seems that those people are written off as disposable by the media. Compare that to the terrorist attack of 9/11 in which fewer people died and ask yourself why they are receiving all the attention? WHY are these human beings valued higher? Shouldn't all unnecessary losses of innocent human lives be treated as of equal value?

For the safety of the patient a non-timid caregiver/advocate can make a difference between life and death. When called upon, be this non-timid caregiver!

Before a patient is released from the hospital, a Case Manager may get quite involved, especially in situations where the patient to be released is expected to require continued help and support. In all cases, I have found the Case Manager to be extremely helpful and dedicated. Invariably they have made the transition from hospital to home or institution as smooth as one could possibly expect. Here is one profession, which is and has been very valuable to both patient and caregiver.

Applying for Social Security Disability

Disability as defined by Social Security has some very strict rules. In order to be considered disabled, you basically must be unable to do any substantial work because of a medical condition and such medical condition must have lasted, or be expected to last, at least one year or be expected to result in your death. There is another requirement. You must have paid Social Security (FICA) taxes at least 5 of the 10 years immediately before your disability.

If you read that definition, one would assume that if you cannot work and you have an incurable disease, such as MS, which by its nature is going to last more than one year and as a consequence it will definitely result in your death, approval would be a given. Not a chance! Social Security doesn't want to approve any disability payment at least that was our experience. Initial claims for Social Security Disability are rarely approved, more than 60% are denied.

They say it takes about 3 to 5 months to get a decision and that depends allegedly on how much time it takes for them to get your medical records and other evidence.

We had everything prepared and submitted all the documentation. It took them about 3 months to turn down the request. Allegedly my wife wasn't disabled according to their research, as a matter of fact, according to the interview they conducted with her primary care physician, she didn't even have MS. We requested a transcript of the interview with her physician, but that was considered confidential and they wouldn't release the transcript. When I pointed out the fact that this physician had passed away three years prior to the interview, I asked them if there was any possibility for me to speak to the individual who had conducted the interview and shake his hand since I had never had the opportunity to meet a person who had a hot line to GOD allowing conversations with people long after they passed away. In spite of the fact that the taxpayers of this country are their employers, their attitude is strange. They don't have any sense of humor and they appeared to be insulted by my doubting their thorough and complete work. They didn't understand that I was impressed, not with the results, but with the ability to conduct this interview.

You now go through another process called "reconsideration." We pointed out all the weird statements they made in the original denial and submitted further proof that she had MS and was unable to work. It was turned down again because the contention was that Phyllis was able to lift 5 pounds. How they arrived at that is a mystery because she couldn't even lift a spoon.

Experience shows, that this process may result in an approval, however the chances are close to "NIL." I always wondered what would happen if a disabled person was brought in on a stretcher and a team of specialists were to confirm that the patient will probably die of a heart attack when they approve the disability claim. Would they approve or disapprove the application?

I then spoke to an attorney and he wasn't particularly interested in the case because Social Security pays a certain amount (A percentage of the retroactive benefits not to exceed a stipulated dollar amount) which doesn't allow for the attorney to make his monthly payments on his Rolls Royce or Bentley. I talked the attorney into taking the case with the promise that I would do all the research. All he had to do is represent my wife in court. He agreed. I went to work and collected all the information, how other cases had been presented and eventually put a pretty good case together. This took about 18 months. Eventually we went to Federal Court and our attorney presented his case. In court, only the attorney and the claimant, who was in a wheelchair, was allowed to be before the administrative judge, I was thrown out. What an ego crusher! That lasted about 3 minutes before I was called in because the judge couldn't understand what my wife was saying and couldn't even hear her responses. I was now called in and recognized as the official caregiver. The upshot was, we won the case and my wife was paid retroactively to the original application date.

There are legal practices soliciting this business. You can see their commercials on TV but they normally only accept a case after the patient has been turned down following the "reconsideration" step.

If you are applying for Social Security Disability, **don't give up!** You must not falter. If you or your patient is **truly** disabled, you are entitled and eventually you will overcome.

Feelings
(from positive to negative)

Feelings are created through a reaction to imaginary and perceived events. That in itself is further complicated by the personalities involved. Psychiatrists make a living identifying these different traits.

Remember a few key sentences: The caregiver is the healthy one, you are lucky! Patient and caregiver frustrations, unless controlled by the healthy one, will lead to conflict! Caregiver and patient priorities are totally different; caregiver has to deal with two priorities, the patient only with one. It may have a tendency to create conflicts!

In this description I want to elaborate more on common views and misconceptions fueled by flawed data obtained by studied people and so called "experts" in the field or through surveys and interviews with some people. Some of the data comes from self-serving organizations such as pharmaceutical companies and associations allegedly supporting people with certain disabilities. Listening to or reading their data, information and recommendations as to how to cope with a myriad of problems may lead to caregiver guilt feelings, resentment and even depression, when before, without all this wonderful data, they were coping admirably with their job or responsibilities. Patient resentment is understandable; I will allude to it in connection with potential caregiver problems.

If we were to develop a chart for all problems related to caregiver/patient interaction, it would show a scale on the left side going from the bottom to the top representing Zero problems/togetherness at the bottom and 100% problems and total disconnect at the top. Obviously to enjoy the most ideal relationship between two people is to be at the bottom of the chart, the NO PROBLEM/TOGETHERNESS spot. At the far right, is the departure of the caregiver and total abandonment of the patient and anything in between; how can you prevent reaching the far right of the scale?

There are two approaches. My wife's and the one practiced by the rest of the world.

I will describe my wife's simple solution to the elimination of any caregiver problem with the patient. Several of my friends and neighbors have expressed their amazement about my commitment and dedication to my wife and never complaining about anything. One of my friends inquired about the secret to our perfect marriage. In order to understand her concept, reading the section "what happened along the way" may be helpful. When she was still physically capable of doing pretty much anything, we traveled extensively. On one of our "Visit National Parks and Monuments" trips, we went to the Grand Canyon, where we rented some mules and descended to the bottom of the canyon. On the way down, suddenly her mule stumbled almost throwing my wife off. Once the animal recovered, my wife got off the animal, stood in front of the mule, looked the animal in the eyes and said, "That's once!" She then re-mounted and we proceeded on our way. After about a ten minute ride, the animal stumbled for a second time. My wife repeated her previous exercise and this time said to the animal, "This is twice!" We hadn't gone very far when the mule stumbled for the third time. My wife again dismounted, took a revolver out of her purse and shot the animal.

I was dismayed and yelled, "What is wrong with you? Are you nuts killing this beautiful animal?" She turned around, looked at me and said, "That's once!"

Since then I have been solidly on the very far side of the "No PROBLEM/TOGETHERNESS" scale and we have had the most wonderful and peaceful relationship. The thought of any guilt feeling, resentment or depression never entered my mind. One of the most important issues to maintain a trouble free relationship is to have the ability to joke around. Laughter is good medicine.

Now let's tackle the more common approach.

The very first question you as a caregiver must ask of yourself is the following: "If I were in the position of the patient, a helpless person, would I be terribly depressed and annoyed if I were abandoned? Go a step further and think of yourself being dumped into a nursing home and visualize the "attentive" care you will receive. If you have a hard time imagining things, visit a nursing home around lunch time and sit there observing the whole process. This exercise may help you move a few notches toward the left side of the chart.

Personalities are influenced by a multitude of conditions and some of the steps I am describing will have no impact no those who consider "abandonment" as being the ideal situation. Those are the people you see and hear about in the daily newscasts. An example is a recent story of a shopper stepping over a dying woman in order to reach for that item on SALE. I really don't believe those individuals in the story would be your choice for a caregiver.

Then you have recommendations from alleged experts who have arrived at their expertise not by actually performing the work of a caregiver, but by sponsored studies and surveys. Some of these surveys are strictly structured to come up with answers that serve their purpose, like "1–Do you suffer from high blood pressure?" YES/NO/DON'T KNOW. "2–Are you in favor of reducing sodium in X Product if it reduces your blood pressure?" YES/NO/DON'T KNOW. Further questions are then structured to basically come up with an answer that low sodium products are favored. If you never suffered from High Blood Pressure would you answer – NO or hell NO to question 2? It is possible, but unlikely. How many people even answer surveys honestly? How many people have enough knowledge about certain issues to answer them correctly? What is most galling is that most of the surveys that come in the mail have a donation coupon attached to the survey with a "please do not detach" note printed on the fold. Does that mean that if you do not send a donation you already demonstrated that you are not in agreement with whatever support they expect from you and they discard your survey?

I received a survey with this question: "Are you in favor of reducing funds for Homeland Security and expose our country to potential terrorist attacks?" Isn't that a loaded question?

How do you deal with the imaginary and perceived problems which may trigger a caregiver guilt trip, resentment or depression?

The personality of the patient before the affliction must be taken into account. Was the individual a kind, caring and a non-confrontational individual or a severely unbalanced and unpredictable person or just plain mean? Even in the latter case, becoming a "non-resentful" caregiver is achievable in spite of a higher degree of potential abuse which the caregiver would have to endure. Your own personality will form your demeanor. If you are a selfish person and only see things from your point of view, reaching the far left of the scale, "NO PROBLEM" by both patient and caregiver, can become an insurmountable obstacle unless the caregiver makes a true attempt at a necessary character modification. Only a strong minded and determined person will OVERCOME.

When healthy, we cherish one trait more than anything else; it is called "independence." That's why criminals are deprived of it when jailed. We think for ourselves and do whatever comes to mind, be it good, bad or indifferent. In the vast majority of the cases we don't need help for standard day to day chores. With the onset of a disabling disease or a sudden change as a result of an accident or by a war inflicted major wound, that situation changes totally. The patient is keenly aware of the major change from the way it used to be. While the same is true for slowly diminishing capabilities as we age, we seem to have the ability to fake it much better. The change occurs at a time when everybody can recognize this white haired old person and expects less.

As a result, the caregiver has to deal with a somewhat erratic and confused patient and will hear such statements as, "Can't you see I need help?" when the patient runs into a situation which used to be easy, like opening a soda can. If you are observant enough and anticipate the problem when he/she is reaching for a soda can and open it for him/her, you may get the opposite statement such as, "Why are you doing everything, do you think I am a cripple?" The potential caregiver resentment will be, "I can't do right for this patient who doesn't appreciate anything" or you may express your own frustration in some more flowery language.

As a caregiver you must understand that the patient lost a freedom enjoyed before and from time to time will express a high degree of frustration. Don't try to attribute deleterious motives to these expressions! Just ignore "unfriendly" comments and keep on doing what your observations dictate you to do. Over time, your consistency and non-reaction will eventually be accepted by the patient.

There will be many situations when the patient will "lecture" you about certain things, especially when you are taking over a function the patient used to be responsible for, like paying the bills. You may perceive the following as a lecture. "When the bills come I always opened the envelope and pay right away. By the way, I made certain notations in the checkbook, you should do the same." You may have a different style. You may want to pay on-line and not write any checks or you may want to make payments on the due date so that you earn interest on your money. You may think, "Butt out, I am now doing it" and get bent out of shape. The best approach is to say, "Dear, I am grateful for your input and I thank you." Say it in a loving voice and don't be sarcastic. At no time did the patient do anything but show love and affection.

Caregiver time management capabilities will have an impact. It is quite common to hear expressions from the patient such as, "What are you doing? How come you are always too busy to do things for me? Frustration is at its peak! Your time has to be managed differently and includes many other aspects, all related to taking care of the patient but in a more remote fashion from the patients perspective. The fact that you are preparing a meal for the patient and cannot change the bed sheet at the same time, escapes the patient. Another issue is the fact that the patient, in all probability, was previously employed. If he or she had a stressful job, did he or she have a commute of more than 30 minutes? If the answer is YES, then you should realize that during that commute some of the frustration was being vented either by quietly insulting someone in the privacy of the car, cutting off the driver considered a pain or do anything else that would shed some of the frustrations of the day. This venting time is not available to the disabled person who is either stuck in the wheelchair or in bed. You become the punching bag – you are right there, who else? Ignore it again, it isn't a personal insult.

Most people don't understand time. You may say, "well that is ridiculous." Do you know, a healthy couple has 48 hours per day? If both sleep 8 hours, 32 hours are left. Assume a total of 3 hours dedicated to food preparation, eating and personal hygiene, that leaves a grand total of 26 hours to do whatever is desirable or required. Much can be accomplished in 26 hours per day.

Compare this to the patient/caregiver time relationship. A severely disabled patient contributes 0 hours; therefore the available time is diminished immediately by 13 hours. The 13 hours of available time by the caregiver is reduced by a minimum of 4 hours a day for attending to the many mandatory requirements of the patient. All duties which were split by the couple now must be handled by the caregiver in the 9 hours available. When a patient has to see a doctor that time now comes out of the caregiver's allotment. Previously one could go to the doctor and the other was attending to other chores during that time. In essence, the 26 hours of available time by the couple prior to the affliction is reduced by two thirds to approximately 8 hours on average. With only one third of the time available, the caregiver has to be a tremendously skilled time manager to achieve the required results or has to be fairly wealthy to buy the time. Only a few people are in the wealthy category because the disease of the patient not only zaps time but money too.

Let's assume you have already reached a level somewhere close to the left side of the scale. You are the understanding type and ask the patient for their desired meal. The patient tells you and you comply. If you are lucky, what you put together is perfect and the patient praises the meal. There is also the possibility, after a few bites, the patient decides enough is enough, no more. You could be resentful; after all, you went out of your way to produce the desired meal. What's the matter, how ungrateful, you mumble something like, "I'll be damned if I make another meal," right?

Has your mood ever impacted what you feel like eating? Has your mood changed after a few bites because suddenly you just don't feel like eating whatever you thought you wanted? Why can't that happen to the patient? God forbid the patient now has another request because the hunger wasn't satisfied, what would your reaction be?

These are all real examples, which could make you resentful. Remember, in order to reach the left side of the scale, "No Problem" by both parties, encourage the patient to say whatever, no matter how annoying it may be and accept everything, knowing that at no time is it intended to be a personal attack on the function you are performing as a caregiver.

By learning to keep our cool over many years, we have achieved the ultimate joint "No PROBLEM" level. Finally humor is absolutely mandatory.

Each morning when I start the new day, one of my first questions is, "Do you have any pain?" When I hear the response, "You are the pain...." I am happy! I respond with a new insult of my own and we both laugh because it is the beginning of one more perfect day in our life, a day we have every intention of enjoying to the fullest.

Let me address some of the many recommendations that are available for Caregivers. Some are very sensible, others are almost an insult. Most deal with avoiding potential depression and how to prevent shortening the caregiver's lifespan because of the care giving job. I can imagine an unemployed worker being depressed, but someone who actually does a very commendable job should find it rather rewarding, not depressing. One recommendation, which I find insulting and if not insulting, definitely very selfishly motivated is the fact that you suddenly may have to accept becoming a caregiver. You better accept it; the person suffering from the consequences of the problem obviously has no choice but to accept it. Show your strength, remember you are still healthy.

It is also recommended that you educate yourself about your loved one's disease or the wound he or she needs to contend with in order to avoid depressions. Do you really need that recommendation? When you buy one of the new electronic devices and the little booklet that comes with it attempts to educate you in 15 different languages, would you be depressed if the booklet wouldn't be included in the box?

Another wonderful recommendation is that you better get organized otherwise you may get depressed again. Frustrated maybe, depressed NO. There is no question that one has to re-arrange his/her life in order to cope with the different duties. When we accept a new job, any job, don't we have to adjust ourselves to a new environment and get organized? If you can't deal with it, do you get depressed? I would assume you may get depressed after they fire you for incompetence. Why would a Caregiving job be any different? Another one of the recommendations is making sure to leave some time to relax. As part of the Caregiving job you have duties that automatically will distract you and relax you like cooking or meal preparation for yourself or the patient. If you don't know how to boil water for a cup of coffee, it's a good time to learn and increase your versatility. Organize and streamline your bill paying process. Use e-mails to contact people in order to reduce telephone calls and shop on-line. This lets you control your time usage much more efficiently. If you need a short distraction and have to use the US Mail service, drive to your nearest mail-box, I don't mean the one at the end of your driveway. Prepare a daily "TO DO LIST." It takes a short time to prepare but you save time because you stay focused and accomplish tasks much faster. Innovate, change and constantly look for more efficient ways of accomplishing things. Study your patient carefully because you will get ideas on how to be better and better.

The researchers feel sleep is very important. My body is way ahead of the researchers. When I am tired, I fall asleep no matter where I am. Sometimes I sleep for 15 minutes and my batteries are recharged for another 2 hours. The researchers contend that sleep disruption can lead to insanity. I guess I should be insane by now, because when I was in a war zone, the opposing guys didn't care about my sleep and they launched surprise attacks. Even with bombs exploding, I adapted Now I sleep 2 or 3 times during the day and I don't mind if my wife calls me at three o'clock in the morning because she suffers from some kind of a pain. Big Deal!

Another suggestion is to ask for help. Of course if you can find someone who is truly willing to help you, that is terrific. But what is frustrating and sometimes depressing is when you ask organizations you believe are there to help and they make you run from pillar to post. If you are successful, bless you, you have the patience to persevere. Personally I don't really like to try, because I get more frustrated when I have to deal with insensitive people.

Another weird view is that one should delay important decisions. I have never heard that procrastination or delay is a viable option to reduce depression. The most important issue is to deal with obstacles and overcome them. Confront your problem; you will not have much time to get depressed.

Let me now address something I will call FEAR. In *Appendix A* you can find a front page article which was printed in the Sarasota Herald Tribune on December 20, 2009 titled "Journey of Love" and written by their staff reporter Mr. Billy Cox. He wrote a very inspirational article based on our experience. I received many comments regarding this article, most very positive but then there were some negative ones. The negative ones came from people afflicted by MS. The comments were very valuable because they showed that people afflicted by non-curable diseases which seem to gradually get worse and worse over time have to deal with something human beings are not really trained for. We all know that from time to time we will encounter an unpleasant health related problem, be it a cold, a more serious sickness or even an accident. That will become a low point, or a bad memorable event at that time. We will see a doctor or have an operation and we will eventually recover and feel better. A better situation than the one left behind. Even people who have limbs amputated begin to adjust, either through artificial limbs or people who just learn to cope with it, like people who lost their arms and started to paint with their mouth. The accident was the low point; the recovery was on an uphill slope. People with ever worsening disabilities reach a temporary plateau or a new low point on a daily basis and know that there is no recovery, or an uphill slope. It just will not get better until there is some major medical breakthrough. A description of the slow evolutionary process described in the article reminds people and it can cause fear. Some of those people commented that if they get closer to the point that my wife has experienced, they sure hope they have the strength to take some pills and exit this world. If people are truly inclined to do that, the question has to be, "Why wait, you already lost all hope?"

Others commented that they would not want their spouse to become a slave of the particular disease and lose their own life. Really? Does that mean they really didn't mean their marriage vows? If you think along those lines, you should never enter into a marriage contract where you make a commitment to your spouse before GOD that you will be around until death will you part. I was truly amazed by some of these comments, especially since I attended a military school and we were taught from the very beginning that you will never abandon a comrade in arms. I would say a commitment to your spouse should be no different. Anything else is just plain selfishness.

I am leaving the most depressing thought for the last. The experts, individuals with PHD's and professors from prestigious universities, warn that one of the biggest problems caregivers face is the fact that they are constantly grieving.

They contend that certain actions or tasks highlight how the patient's disability or illness severely affects the caregiver. A particular report used the following language, "the patients rob them of a brighter future."

I would not be surprised to see certain individuals who would be negatively impacted by taking care of a family member. Those individuals probably would grieve eternally when confronted with any serious challenge, be it a divorce, the loss of their job or the death of a person they loved. To some of these, suicide is their escape.

I feel the luminaries who publish these views are concentrating on the negative, in essence the minority, rather than the majority who are realists. The contention that a patient robs them of a brighter future is actually a ridiculous statement. One could easily turn this around and say that caring for a patient saved the individual from a terrible future. Obviously, we have no idea what the future has in store for us.

The fact remains; the caregiver is the healthy one, which is a gift from GOD. Thank God and be positive.

Take a look at *Appendix B* and you will see a part of a speech in which we are recreating a joyful experience in a very imaginative way to bring a memory to life. The patient's view of this effort is precious and it certainly is far from being depressing for the caregiver.

I find that most of the recommendations made are totally misguided. When you accept a Caregiving job there is no question that it will be a challenge. The Caregiving challenge is a fabulous job with big psychological rewards. To see yourself succeed and make the life of a person, suffering from whatever affliction, more rewarding is a fantastic achievement and you should cherish those moments.

Caregivers and Social Workers

Any caregiver, family member or not, should be aware of a very important issue.

There may come a time when, for whatever reason, you will have to place a call to 911 because the patient has an unusual medical emergency or may have fallen and sustained an injury. The "first responders" upon arrival, in all probability, will decide to take the patient to the emergency room at the closest hospital.

When such a patient arrives at the hospital and is rolled into a treatment room, a number of nurses, aids and medical technicians will show up before the physician can see the patient. Among all the people surrounding the patient, there is a good chance a social worker may also appear to see and talk to the patient. Some of those have shown up wearing a medical robe, as if they wanted to make you believe that they were not social workers.

The purpose is to check if for some reason the disabled patient was brought to the hospital because of some abuse or neglect by the caregiver or other family member. Unfortunately abuse is occurring much too frequently in today's society and has been well documented, thus this is a necessary service being provided to protect helpless patients from such an occurrence. The general concept is very commendable and unfortunately necessary.

In my many years of having to deal with situations like these, I have met a significant number of social workers. I found the majority of them doing their job in a professional and correct manner. However, there have been several cases when the social workers did not have the interrogative skills and used lamentable techniques because they received little to no training in how to communicate with patients or caregivers. I always carry a voice recorder around my neck and usually have my camera cell phone ready to record conversations such as these. Over time, our nation has reached a point when well- intentioned programs have gotten out of hand and one must be constantly on guard. As I said before, while we need these individuals to identify abusers, they can cause you unnecessary grief by making irresponsible comments at a time when you could use some friendly support.

Role of Caregiver as Advocate

While this Caregiving book covers an evolutionary process from the patient being basically normal to eventually becoming 100% dependent on a caregiver, the emphasis is mostly directed to the totality of the job and severest side of the disability.

During the evolutionary process, a time may come when the patient, the family and the caregiver, whoever that may be, will reach a decision fork on their road into the future. The choices are as follows: Make a left turn and the patient is moved into an Assisted Living Facility, a regular Nursing Home or a Skilled Nursing Home facility, one that basically handles the more complicated cases, or make a right turn and keep the patient in a familiar environment, the home. This decision fork can be reached at any time along the way and whatever decision is made by the family and the patient is a very personal matter. Having the patient stay in a familiar environment doesn't necessarily mean that the caregiver must now dedicate all his/her time entirely to the patient. Again there will be a number of different options, all of which depend on the degree of the disability, the financial resources available to the patient and most importantly the personality of both the patient and the caregiver. If the patient wants perfection and the caregiver is a perfectionist, it is doubtful that reliance on outside resources may be acceptable no matter what financial resources are available. Basically, if you really want something done right, do it yourself. In my case, I made the decision to accept the fact that life is bound to become more hectic, involved and complicated and without a doubt there will be a need of acquiring the skills to excel. Again this decision is a very personal choice.

There are some very meaningful differences between still being able to work and being totally confined to a facility or your home. In the former case, a handicapped or disabled person, while tremendously "inconvenienced" is still in control of their own fate. They even have laws to help them or protect them (maybe) like ADEA (Age Discrimination in Employment Act of 1967) which prohibits employers from discriminating against workers who are between the ages of 40 and 70 on the basis of age. Then there is ADA (Americans with Disabilities Act of 1990) which prohibits employers from discriminating against qualified disabled workers and requires employers to make reasonable efforts to accommodate the disability of an otherwise qualified individual. Another one is the Civil Rights Acts of 1964 and 1991 which among certain provisions allegedly doesn't allow for discrimination on the basis of a handicap. There are some other laws which cover those that are disabled but still working. There is NO LAW that covers the patient who is totally helpless other than criminal laws when a patient is physically abused by someone or being defrauded.

Those who are disabled and are still working, depending on their financial resources, have access to a number of services for a fee ranging from low to high, depending on the person being retained or hired. You can have shopping done, baby sitting services (licensed services cost more but you still have a 50/50 chance of child abuse), transportation, pet care including walking your pet, probably a surcharge if you have to pick-up what the pet left behind, lawn manicurists (do you like that service?) and the list goes on and on. These services spring into action provided you have some decent income and can afford all these different versions. It does not address those still working with very low income who couldn't afford to pay for all this (most of them). So if a Caregiver HELPER (not Caregiver), be it a friend or family member, absorbs some of these chores or duties, the patient is helped and hopefully the costs are in a range of acceptability. The Caregiver Helper obviously gains experience along the way and will become proficient in a specific area.

Under the circumstances described, those issues associated with the medical environment are usually excluded, like visits to the doctor, having tests performed or dealing with insurance and billing issues. In most instances they are usually still handled by the patient. A service or Caregiver Helper may drive them to the doctor but then sits in the waiting room until the patient re-emerges.

A Caregiver, as I have described, is an individual who competes with the Assisted Living Facility (ALF), the Regular as well as the Skilled Nursing Home. Their services are provided at a steep cost. The services provided by either the institutions or the Caregiver Expert are mandatory because without them, the patient would or could not survive.

The Caregiver Expert now fulfills the same or better role on behalf of the patient at a minimal cost. Maybe someone moves in to save their rent and uses the funds, be it social security or disability income, to get fed. One can't say it is totally free except if the Caregiver Expert is a husband or wife.

If a patient were to contract for a variety of these services at a cost of $10-35 per hour, he or she would need a full time accountant to keep things straight. The chances are that when one makes a comparison between this approach and an ALF or Nursing Home, the latter may actually be more cost effective but not necessarily better. There is one significant difference between a loving Caregiver and the institutions. The institutions will minimally or NOT defend the interests of a patient. They will contact a family member or guardian who may have to make decisions on behalf of the patient based on insufficient or unreliable data and thus remotely and unbeknownst to him or her, doom the survivability of the patient.

There is no question, a patient who truly needs 24/7 attention, when given a choice, will prefer to remain in a familiar environment, usually their own home, rather than play Russian roulette and entrust his or her fate to the slippery and greedy arms of an institution. The Caregiver Expert is a permanent Health Care Surrogate and uses his Power of Attorney or some special releases all the time. In essence, the Caregiver becomes the patient without the disease. At one point, my wife recognized that fact. We were on our way to the doctor's office for a previously scheduled appointment. While driving along, she asked me; "Why am I going to the doctor? I don't have a problem except going through the nightmare of getting dressed and being lifted out of bed in order to be transferred to the wheelchair." She continued on and said; "I sit there in my wheelchair listening to you and the doctor talk. When you are done, you drive me back home. I feel like the horse in your Russian merchant story." I had to laugh! Ironically, in a way, she was correct.

Somehow our medical system moved away from the doctor visiting the patient to the patient having to get up and visit the doctor, in spite of the fact that it can become a real challenge for the severely disabled. Doctors will go to the hospital; however the home, which is the "hospital" for the severely disabled is off limits. It only demonstrates that severely disabled people are in fact being discriminated against, maybe not conscientiously.

For those who are interested in the "horse analogy", here is the story.

In the horse and buggy days a Russian merchant had to make a trip from Moscow to Kiev. He searched for a driver who knew his way to Kiev and hired him. When they started the trip, the merchant was comfortably seated in the buggy when the trail was going uphill to get over a significant elevation. The driver asked the merchant to get out and help push the buggy since the horse was old and not as strong as it used to be. The merchant complied. As soon as the trail leveled out, the merchant jumped back in. But as they progressed, the trail went up and down and the driver repeatedly told the merchant to either push the buggy uphill or hold the buggy back so it wouldn't run the horse over on the downhill side. After a number of these episodes, the merchant finally stopped the driver and said, "I know why I am going to Kiev, I have to complete a business transaction, I know why you are going to Kiev, you know the way, but why in the world did we have to bring the horse?"

In the Caregiver Advocate role one must handle everything. The main objective is the physical and financial wellbeing of the patient. Then there all of the tasks that had been handled by the patient before he or she became disabled. It is an endless stream of items such as nutrition, hygiene, the administration of medicine, banking, bill paying, sending out birthday cards etc.

The Caregiver Advocate role is not really understood by the majority and sometimes not even by the physician's office staff. The following is an example of what can happen. It became quite clear to me how little the role of a caregiver is understood when I needed to write a letter about a billing issue regarding some service allegedly performed on behalf of my wife. Obviously I had to identify my wife by name so that the office staff could investigate the charge.

She had been a long time patient of this doctor and the staff knew that my wife was not capable of talking, reading and writing. In spite of it, the response was addressed to my wife for "privacy" reasons. Their file was full of copies of my Power of Attorney, but allegedly, that had no bearing.

Since the response was not complete and did not really answer the original question, I had no choice but to send a follow-up letter requesting a proper response in order to resolve the disputed charge. We never received a response and when a renewal for her prescription was called in by the pharmacy, the pharmacy was informed that this particular physician was no longer the patient's doctor. My wife and I were never informed of their decision or the reason for it. One can only surmise that it was a retaliatory move orchestrated by the office staff for questioning them regarding an alleged charge which turned out not to be valid. It was a $12 charge for a service the doctor's office had never performed but was paid in conjunction with another valid charge. It didn't come to light until the "Explanation of Benefits" from the insurance company arrived. In the end I felt, if the office is that petty, they may need the money more than we do and we just found ourselves another physician. It was a shame, because we lost a terrific physician as a result of a problem with his office staff. You may feel, why did I not talk to the physician directly? I explained that in "**Relationship with the Medical Professionals.**" The office staff is a very important part of the overall Physicians Practice and if they want to make your life miserable, they sure can do a wonderful job. An effort to expose them to win a battle over twelve dollars could be counterproductive and actually be dangerous to the patient when faced with an emergency. Looking for another physician is a safer route to follow.

The whole issue of long term Caregiver liabilities varies with state laws. Some states like NY have laws which limit liabilities for Caregivers, but even then it is left to some loose interpretations. If a full time Caregiver gets to a point that he or she feels totally overwhelmed and wants to commit a patient to a nursing home and the patient refuses to go, that patient is entitled to a court hearing and its consequences and delays.

What happens if a Caregiver becomes incapacitated and cannot perform his/her duties any longer? He or she can ask a court for help in finding a new setting for the patient. A Caregiver should make provisions in the event of his or her death. Thomson Reuters (Quickfinder.thomson. com or 800-510- 8997) has an excellent manual called "Social Security & Medicare" which is regularly updated and covers Social Security, Medicare, Medicaid and Eldercare Insurance. I would highly recommend the acquisition of this guide for a thorough coverage of the many options and variables associated with the care of a disabled person and those of advanced age and not necessarily disabled yet.

Earlier I mentioned that as a Caregiver you will and must rely heavily on the Power of Attorney, at least you may think you can without a problem. It isn't that simple. For instance, if the disabled person still wants to participate in the democratic process and vote, you must present paperwork demonstrating that the person will need a permanent absentee ballot (not in all states). The absentee ballot is signed by the disabled person or marked with an X and an authorized witness must then sign and attest to the veracity of the signature. This is in lieu of being notarized. Some insurance companies, even with a Power of Attorney in the patient's file, still demand some of their own forms to be submitted before you can discuss insurance matters of the patient with them. It is the "privacy" that they are protecting. On the internet anybody can buy all the information about any person in this country, even the most private information, but you can't discuss an insurance claim with the insurance company unless they are in the possession of a release. Not only is it frustrating, but in some cases it is outright ridiculous. One insurance company I have dealt with must have about 17 copies of her Power of Attorney and somehow they can never find it or maybe they have people who can't read. Credit Card companies also can give you a real hard time in spite of the fact that all the correct data is being provided. Many times they demand to speak to the patient which can become a real problem, because this patient, my wife. can only whisper, if that. I am only mentioning this so you will be aware of how frustrating your life as a Caregiver can be, not because of the patient but because you must deal with so many ridiculous and illogical rules written by people who have nothing better to do than make your life miserable.

National Support Organizations

There are many organizations promoting themselves as being dedicated to help those afflicted by many of the debilitating diseases like, ALS, Alzheimer's, Cancer, Diabetes, Kidney diseases, Heart related, Multiple Sclerosis, United Fund and on and on. These organizations solicit donations and distribute the money in different ways. There are a smaller number of alleged support organizations for Caregivers, also soliciting donations. The expressions such as "All that glitters is not gold", "Buyer beware", "Common sense is not so common" and ""Men willingly believe what they wish" apply to the above mentioned entities. Organizations that provide, for a fee, a large number of varied commercial Caregiving services for are quite extensive. You make your choice and you or your insurance pays whatever is stipulated for the service requested. These organizations do not solicit donations.

This book does not intend to duplicate or regurgitate information which can be easily obtained through the internet or from the mountains of literature many of these organizations provide. They also keep and provide a long list of "Volunteer" groups, plus county and state social services and their telephone numbers which can be approached for help. I will look at the benefits and drawbacks of these organizations and raise a number of questions. Most, not all, are mainly interested in fund raising to provide researchers the resources in order to find the ever elusive cure to the particular disease or at least come up with some medication which supposedly will improve the patient's lifestyle. Some of them organize seminars to educate those interested in learning more about these diseases or where information for items of interest are provided, like recent discoveries or improvements, while soliciting more donations. Getting any financial help from these "mammoth donation solicitation entities" may become a neat trick and in some instances involves more paperwork than what is required to get a multimillion dollar mortgage approved. For example, I approached one of the organizations to see what would be involved in order to get a "wheelchair cushion." They mailed me a six sheet package which had to be submitted to them. The forms were necessary in order for them to evaluate if my wife, based on her medical history, current condition and the family financial resources may be eligible to sit on something soft. If after their committees determine that she may have a cushion, one has to get a prescription from the doctor. Who knows how much time would elapse before one could possibly be rewarded with the cushion. During that time, that part of the body would be sufficiently conditioned to find a concrete slab soft enough.

The endless stream of personal information solicited in order to qualify for anything, which is nothing more than a king-size intrusion into your privacy cannot possibly be rewarded with a cushion, but that is just my view.

In analyzing these organizations, there is quite a difference of how much of that money is actually allocated to helping those afflicted by the different diseases and how much money is retained for "Administrative" expenses like compensation packages. When carefully reviewing their financial statements, one can find compensation monies for employees or consultants distributed throughout the organization. In essence these expenses are being camouflaged under a number of headings. I can't help but ask this question. If such an organization accumulates huge amounts of money in order to find a cure for those people afflicted by the disease, what kind of incentive does the leadership of such an organization have to encourage researchers to find the cure that will make the organization extinct? Wouldn't that wipe out their generous compensation packages? What incentives do the research labs have who are the beneficiaries of these multi-million dollar grants to really find **THE CURE**? Maybe some pieces a long the way to show that progress is being made, but the **BIG ONE**? Remember, these people are encouraged to find answers to these diseases which are called "Orphan Diseases." Should they find a blockbuster pill, how much money can a pharmaceutical company possibly make based on the smaller amount of people who would need such medication? I am not a cynic, I am a realist! The organizations that raise money for research grants at least do provide a service with the intent to find "improvements." A number of organizations established to help caregivers cannot show true value. Their slogans are quite impressive however when you really study the services they portray as being valuable in meeting their mission goals you can only come to one conclusion, they are grossly overstated and more self-serving. As an active caregiver for a quarter of a century, the fact that such an organization will provide me with information as to how many people are caring for people over 50 or what the household income is of those being cared for is totally meaningless to my job as a caregiver. How can they truly portray their mission as improving the quality of the caregiver or their patient? How does that improve in any shape or form my job as a caregiver? Nothing I have read in all their literature would have been of any assistance to me from the day I entered the field of Caregiving as a neophyte and progressed all the way to achieve my professional status as a caregiver expert. What if someone was to create a tax-exempt foundation called "**N**ational **O**rganization **F**or **O**ur **O**verweight **D**ads" with a mission statement of decreasing the weight of dads without ever telling you **HOW**. A curious person would contact them and ask them how to achieve such a fabulous objective. As a result of your question, you are bombarded with slick slogans and useless statistics only to realize that their only intent was to raise money and not provide any support. You missed the acronym of the organization, i.e. "**NOFOOD.**" Following that recipe, anyone eliminating food will succeed. Did they deceive you? YES! That was the intent! Who do you really believe will be the true beneficiaries of your donations, the people that need the help or the members of the fundraising organization? Remember the expression "All that glitters is not gold!" The tax code allows these donations to be deducted from the "donators" tax return. How many of these "donators" are truly doing this for the noble reason to make sure that those in distress will see a better future and suffer less? Many, but not all!

In the many years of dealing with a variety of organizations, I have found for profit business organizations much more helpful than the name brand "Support Groups." The business organizations can be approached to provide services at a lower cost. For certain supplies they may be willing to quote the equivalent of wholesale prices by adding additional items for free, in essence resulting in a quantity discount. Your physician can be approached for "samples" to reduce your prescription costs or direct you to specific pharmacies which will dispense certain medications for free or highly discounted. For that commercial enterprise these are loss leaders but they are compensated by being able to attract people to buy items which are quite profitable to them.

In order to provide some examples of how support organizations respond, I wrote a number of letters to different organizations. I used the description of their services in which they explain how the donations collected are used to support those afflicted by their respective diseases. All my requests usually addressed specific equipment needs. I solicited their recommendations as to what equipment would best accommodate a patient's requirements and if they could provide contacts or true educational material. I was not interested in statistical information or data one can obtain from the internet printed on their flyers. At no time did I request any financial assistance. The vast majority never responded, those that answered varied a great deal but in general were quite evasive and only gave several telephone numbers of Social Services and Elder Care programs to contact. There was only one organization that went out of their way to truly be helpful and find the appropriate equipment, which I questioned them about and that organization was the ALS organization. (ALS stands for Amyotrophic Lateral Sclerosis often called Lou Gehrig's disease).

Appendix F: Shows a copy of a letter I wrote to the MS Centers of Florida Foundation. This was in response to a letter and donation request my wife received at Christmas in 2004 (Good timing!), included was some of their literature. Since I didn't know of their existence, I carefully read all the material.

After they received my letter, they called me in order to provide me with a bunch of telephone numbers for Social Services, Elder Care programs and, believe it or not, the MS Society. They also gave me an assurance of support for more numbers, should I need them.

This conversation with an official from this organization made me realize that as a poor immigrant who had to learn English after my arrival in this wonderful country I apparently didn't have an understanding of the **TOTAL** meaning of words.

In their literature they are saying and I quote, "With your help united we stand to develop programs and <u>deliver</u> care and <u>support</u> to those <u>afflicted</u> with and <u>affected</u> by Multiple Sclerosis." It also states and I quote again, "Service Delivery: Establishment of programs to help provide both medical and non- medical services."

Until then, I interpreted words by the more frequently used meanings such as:

Delivery = "to carry and turn over to the intended recipient things such as letters or goods." They used the other meaning such as "to give forth in words, utter or pronounce"

Support = "to maintain, as a person, family, or institution, by supplying with things necessary to existence." They used the other meaning such as "to sustain or withstand without giving way or bear with fortitude."

Afflicted = "to give, as pain which is continued or of some permanence." They used the other meaning such as "to the mind, to humble, to trouble."

Affected = "to affect the mind or body." They used the other meaning such as "to act upon, to produce an effect or change upon, to influence."

Finally I quote, "the success of our plans depend in large measure by the generosity of our donors… individuals like you."

Their needs are stated as follows:

$450,000 to establish in house staff while generating support for ongoing programs and initiatives.

$250,000 for expansion of social services and other important non-medical activities.

$150,000 to match resources in hand for ongoing operations.

$ 75,000 to initiate a financial counseling program for MS patients.

$ 50,000 to complete a currently unavailable census profile of the MS population in Florida to provide an accurate picture of the size, status and needs of the population.

$ 45,000 for office equipment and space.

If after reading all these requirements you feel the need to provide your financial support, you should also dedicate significant resources to cans of "Dehydrated Water" to assure yourself of a sufficient supply in case of an emergency. For those who do not know how to use a can of dehydrated water, following are the instructions. "Open can, add water and drink!"

They describe all kinds of wonderful services using the English language skillfully, success of which depends in large measure by the generosity of donors like my MS afflicted wife. I used to donate to a large selection of "charitable" organizations. After carefully analyzing many, I have become extremely selective and prefer to help those in real need. At least seeing a face brighten up with a big smile is worth more than a tax deduction.

Appendix G: shows a copy of the 2nd follow-up letter I wrote to the National Family Caregivers Assoc. which is self-explanatory *Appendix H:* shows an e-mail in which my wife inquired about a program called "**Easing Daily Life**" as promoted by the Multiple Sclerosis Association of America. The program is described as follows and I quote, "**Easing Daily Life** provides products and services that assist clients with their day-to-day needs and comfort. Requested equipment is shipped and loaned to clients at no charge (certain income requirements apply, as well as limit on the number of items borrowed). These products increase comfort, safety and/or mobility." My wife needed a hospital bed for a short time. She had never borrowed anything from them; therefore the part about the limit of items borrowed didn't apply to her. My wife's e-mail and the response are self-explanatory. At least they responded. In the end we had to buy one in order for us to be able to effectively move her from one location to the other. Eventually we will donate it to a true charitable organization. After reading this segment, you can go to *Appendix F, G & H* in order to read the letters and the e-mails. You can reach your own conclusion.

Current Condition

Physical Capabilities: On a scale from 1 to 10, one being mildly impaired and ten being severely impacted, she is currently rated a physical nine. She can bend her right arm somewhat but has trouble lifting the arm, it's too heavy. She can barely move some fingers on her right hand. She has little motion control of her right hand, which is referred to as "spasticity". If she would attempt to hold a spoon with one of those straps around her wrist, the chances are about 99.9% that she would drop whatever is on the spoon or the spoon itself before it would ever reach the intended target, her mouth. The effort would be further complicated by the mere fact that aiming for the mouth becomes a major undertaking.

An MS patient has more than an impaired brain capability due to the scaring caused by Multiple Sclerosis and sheer willpower still cannot overcome the physical damage to the transmission lines, the nervous system. Any attempt to pick up a small piece of chocolate with her fingers would end up in complete failure because it's too small and she just doesn't have the capacity or capability to hold it and move it toward her mouth.

Her left hand is totally useless because the fingers have permanently retracted and the thumb is the only part which still has some movement. She can move her head, she cannot lift her head off the pillow. When she is placed in the power wheelchair and transported in the Van, she is securely buckled up. Sudden swerves, as a consequence of following erratic drivers, will tend to move her from one side to the other in her wheelchair. She will not be able to reposition herself and sit straight, even if her arms are firmly positioned on the armrests. Since her legs have no capacity to push or apply pressure at all, her legs can't assist in any shape or form.

There are a number of skin problems that show up from time to time. Some are fungus related; some problems are rashes, which can be caused when there is a change in medication or a skin infection of some sort. In general terms, she has a beautiful skin and is relatively wrinkle free, even without all the wonderful lotions and cream advertised on TV.

She still has a strong heart. The other organs are performing their duties to the best of their ability. Her liver had some hick-ups several years back but is now performing as expected. Her pancreas is somewhat volatile and I will describe its function and relationship to contribute to a harmonious balance. The left kidney is performing admirably. Her right kidney was almost removed in September 2005 when she had a severe infection. As a result of the skilled work by her Urologist and some additional help from the Almighty, it came back to life and has been carefully monitored and kept infection free for the last 4+ years. Now it is performing as expected. The bladder, it appears has won the number one spot to go first, meaning the muscles which protect us from encountering an embarrassing moment, seem to forget to perform their assigned duty, basically "don't let go!" This led to the introduction of a catheter inserted through the urethra and under normal circumstances has to be changed monthly. For 12 years it worked relatively trouble free. There were several occasions when the bladder or the urinary tract became infected and through the use of antibiotics was cleared up.

Her lung capacity has diminished causing speech problems. It has become difficult for her to exhale with force. This translates into an impaired airflow through her vocal cords consequently reducing the vibrations needed to produce sounds, which can then be shaped by the mouth and tongue into words. Sometimes she goes through the speech motions, moving her lips, but no words exit her mouth.

Being able to communicate with a patient is extremely important, thus this occasional disability can cause damaging delays. Over time I have developed a rather imperfect tool. I watch her facial expressions, I attempt to read her lips and I ask questions to which she answers yes or no. When she formulates her favorite word – "Jerk," I know I have not hit the jackpot yet. Eventually I succeed and we live happily thereafter.

When this whole exercise is done to identify pain, it becomes another problem. Since her senses are impaired, not only does she have a problem verbalizing it, attempting to identify a pain location is almost more difficult then reading her lips. Observations over a long period have made it possible, at least more often than not, for me to locate the area of her complaint. Frequently, even the doctor has been unable to quickly identify the problem. In most instances they rely on my observations to locate the trouble spot.

In essence, an observant Caregiver is extremely valuable to the long-term well being of the disabled person. No doctor or nurse can possibly provide this specialized care unless they are also dedicated almost entirely to that person, something that is highly unlikely.

She suffers from double vision, a very frequent problem for people with MS. I tell her she should be a mail carrier; after all she would be extremely productive since she would be able to read the sender's name and the addressee in one scan. Invariably I will be honored with her loving word, "JERK." From a psychological point of view, it is important to be able to joke around and have her participate in the verbal exchange. It does exercise her brain.

As a result of all this she will feel secure and have the confidence to say what comes to mind without fear of any consequence. The disabled person must be able to shed the fear that the wrong word or expression may have undesirable repercussions. The patient must be 100% confident that their expressions are taken the way they are intended, as healthy HUMOR.

To get corrective glasses is quite an experience. Since tests for glasses mostly depend on ones interpretation of how we view things when the optometrist flips through settings and ask the patient, "which one is better, 1 or 2, then 3 or 4?" By the time she has completed that exercise, influenced by the delayed recognition which is part of a MS affliction, she will end up with glasses allowing her to see traffic lights a mile away while sitting in the back of the Van, but can't see the TV screen on her portable DVD player in front of her.

Her hearing is perfect, when it works. Sometimes her hearing is temporarily impaired, when scaring on her brain temporarily blocks a "transmission line" before the brain finds a new route. It becomes obvious when a phone is held to one ear and she contends the phone isn't working, because she can't hear a thing. When it is then changed to the other ear, she shows off her beaming smile, wondering how the phone got repaired so fast.

Her taste buds have also suffered and she enjoys food more based on memories as to how the food is supposed to taste than actually being able to distinguish terrific food prepared by her private chef, her Caregiver. I have tested that theory by describing the same food in different ways and she will either accept it as delicious or reject it all together. Her mind still works fine.

In general, she is tube fed. She get's the proper amount for her build and weight of a complete nutritional supplement for patients with potential hyperglycemia. Ironically Multiple Sclerosis and Diabetes related disorders of the nervous system (diabetic neuropathy) have similar symptoms so it becomes a question of what came first, the chicken or the egg.

Even if a person shows no signs of diabetes, it is very important to monitor glucose levels. It is a known fact that chronic diseases can have severe emotional effects. This in turn has an impact on the blood pressure and glucose levels. A balancing act must take place in order to avoid a potential roller coaster ride of high glucose readings followed by low glucose levels and the associated mood swings. The balancing act involves insulin, food and intense glucose level testing. It is strange that an MS patient that doesn't really have diabetes will require insulin shots from time to time in order to achieve the proper bodily equilibrium. Exercise is normally another ingredient to reach the proper balance, but for a bed-ridden person, that part becomes meaningless since it cannot contribute much.

As I described at the beginning, my wife is rated a NINE from a physical point of view, but from an emotional perspective she is rated a ONE. Why is that? Absolute trust and confidence in her husband Caregiver. Over time she has learned that no matter what her mood, feelings and concerns may be, nothing will ever impair her relationship with her husband. This confidence gives her such peace of mind that she can concentrate on those issues which are crucial to her welfare.

A loving Caregiver's main task is to perform his or her duties in such a way that the patient retains the desire to live a long life, just like any other healthy person.

Since the mindset of the afflicted person is probably more important than any other effort to OVERCOME, the first order of business is to first accept the diagnosis of a disease and the potential consequences. Not accepting the diagnosis is to start the upcoming future by placing limitations on oneself and immediately inhibit any effort to OVERCOME. If one is consumed by finding causes and fault, you have embarked on a path toward defeat. The outcome of that approach is plain and simple – you will fail in any effort to OVERCOME.

A Typical Day

At this point my wife is totally helpless and needs constant attention. As a Caregiver I don't have to sit next to her for hours on end and hold her hand, but I have to follow a schedule, which will change almost on a weekly basis depending on her ever changing conditions and different requirements. Predicting the weather may be easier and we know how well they do in spite of all the technological marvels at their disposal. The best way to portray it is to describe the typical day.

After she wakes up and before any discussion about sleep, feelings and all those wonderful items we will cover, she wants for me to turn on the news. In spite of her physical condition, she still has a sharp mind and in order to maintain it in tip-top shape, she wants to know who screwed up the world since yesterday. In a heartbeat she can separate the screwballs from the smart ones.

After a "basic inspection" it is followed by the routine diagnostic analysis such as taking her temperature, pulse rate, blood pressure and perform a glucose test. At an advanced state of MS, it is almost mandatory that a glucose test is taken daily. At this stage it has nothing to do whether or not the patient has diabetes. As I said earlier, the body is a total entity and all functions are interrelated. In order to prevent sudden surprises, it is extremely important that all bodily relationships be carefully monitored. One important requirement is the checking of her bodily functions over which she has no control. The color and amount of urine are important indicators of kidney and bladder functions. The stool is another crucial indicator, be it by its absence or when present, by its texture and color. You may have difficulties imagining it now and what may be viewed as gross when you are not the affected party, this view will change overnight if it hits you. It will become extremely important when it is your body which has to be maintained in a condition which will make your life somewhat rewarding.

One of the most important tests is the glucose test. My wife doesn't have the conventional type 2 Diabetes, so why the glucose test? Certain conditions, such as a person confined to bed, will show a higher blood glucose level than normal active people. What you eat has a bearing, but not necessarily just because of higher sugar levels. The glucose monitoring will reveal trends and show if her pancreas is producing an appropriate level of insulin to maintain the required equilibrium. During the last few years, she had several seizures. Right after that, her glucose levels increased drastically. Over a period of several weeks after the seizures and with a lot of attention, her glucose level was brought back to normal. In essence her pancreas was affected by the seizure but eventually started to come back and perform its assigned function, specifically keeping the glucose under control through the production of insulin. During the recovery period, she received a number of insulin shots and then was put back on a pill. A glucose reading below 100 mg/dl is desirable and frequent readings in the area between 100mg/dl and 140 mg/dl represent a "YELLOW" light. Since higher readings may impair the healing of wounds, it is very important to monitor trends. In her case, a higher reading doesn't necessarily mean that her pancreas isn't functioning properly; it could also be as a result of the body not using the hormone effectively or the warning bell of some growing infection in her body. In her condition, there are other issues which have to be checked before giving her an insulin shot.

To a degree, diabetic symptoms are mirror images of the ones associated with those of MS, such as frequent urination. To prevent accidents, she has a catheter in her bladder. Feeling of weakness is already a common occurrence with MS, the extent may differ, a high glucose level will make her sleepier than normal but so will some of her medications. The important issue is that diabetic signs, if left untreated, can progress to diabetic coma and death.

Cleaning of the skin, no matter where, is important but sometimes problematic. The skin is very sensitive to any rubbing. How that is possible is somewhat of a mystery since many of the nerves are severed with MS. Caring for her skin requires the use of certain medicated cleansing products prescribed by her Dermatologist. The intent is to avoid potential infections, especially around the feeding tube. Due to being bedridden, I must protect the skin on her back from the development of a superficial dermal ulcer, therefore every four days, DuoDerm extra thin shields are applied. These are not covered by any insurance and are high priced items. Her legs, arms and hands have to be moved frequently to make sure that they don't get locked in a fixed position. It could be quite painful when one has to lift her out of bed and move her into a wheelchair. In regard to the legs, it is not uncommon for her to complain about a pain in the left leg, which has no feeling. Sometimes she asks that the other leg be straightened out. Since I am mystified by her request, I lift her up so that she can actually see the position of the leg, which is straight as a rail. In spite of the fact that she can actually see the leg differently than what she feels, it does not change her feeling until I carefully massage the leg. Then whatever nerve function is still present sends a message to her brain. Once the new information has been received in the brain, she then feels the leg is beginning to straighten out.

The brain is the most fabulous organ. As a computer professional, the daily observation of how the brain functions is intriguing and frequently astonishing. I wonder if humans will ever be able to imitate, even in small measures, the extensive capabilities of the brain.

My wife is fed through a feeding tube (clinically known as the "PEG-tube"). All her medications are either crushed or diluted and fed through the tube. Some of the medication is available in liquid form. The caloric intake must be monitored in order to provide just the right amount to maintain her weight. The amount of water has to be adjusted based on a variety of conditions including what medication is being administered. Some medications need higher amounts of water otherwise the lack of it could cause some kidney problems. As a healthy person, you may think, this is obvious. People with diseases such as MS may not recognize the fact that they are thirsty.

The availability of the feeding tube gives her an option we don't have. Sometimes I ask my wife to open her mouth so that I can give her the cherry flavored liquid medication. She looks at me and I think I can hear the gears grinding in her brain when she tells me, "No, today put it through the tube."

Each day she is given a nutritional supplement in a quantity intended not to exceed her stipulated caloric level. In addition she is fed items such as applesauce, pudding, ice cream, mashed potatoes, mashed vegetables or tiny pieces of meat, fish or chicken. While I do this, I watch her carefully to make sure she swallowed her food and give her tiny sips of water. This exercise is important for two reasons. She can tolerate some medication better with "solid" food and her throat muscles get some exercise, which also improves her speech.

There are a number of problems with the "feeding tube". The area around the tube must be kept clean and infection free, which is a tricky challenge. In spite of having the balloon inside the stomach properly inflated to provide the seal, it is almost impossible to prevent spillage including stomach acid around the tube. If the patient has to cough for whatever reason, sometimes the content of the stomach is forced out. While the padding around the tube may absorb it, it will have a tendency to burn and irritate the skin causing an infection.

Food, water and crushed or liquid medications have to be introduced slowly or at different times to prevent liquid from spilling out. The tube itself has to be flushed every time in order to keep it clean and not inhibit the normal flow. The tube has to be changed on a regular basis, the longer between changes, the happier the insurance company will be. This is an out-patient procedure performed in the hospital. An experienced caregiver may be properly trained to perform the procedure at home for a fraction of the cost.

The different doctors who she sees routinely have prescribed a combined total of sixteen different medications. Over a period of four years (the last four years) I have been making every attempt to reduce her reliance on some of the medications and have been able to bring it down to 6. None were specifically for MS. In spite of the fact that these medications come with an indicated dosage, I may change the dosage anytime depending on her particular condition or tolerance for certain medications. I have discussed this with the physicians and they have supported my modified treatment plans according to her different conditions. They have given me certain parameters, which I diligently observe. I keep good records.

In our home "hospital" room, I have converted the closet into a small pharmacy. A monitoring system has been installed. It monitors activities around the house and I have a camera pointing at my wife, which is on a 24-hour recording loop. In replaying the recording and observing the actions, one can learn more efficient ways of doing things. I also have a binder where I write down all my observations and actions, this way one can determine patterns over time and be more helpful to the patient, my wife.

The important aspect of my long time experience is the fact that reality is quite different from studied approaches. If a disabled person under the care of a caretaker is admitted to a hospital, invariably you will encounter a negative reaction to any common treatment option which has been revised for personal or efficiency reasons. To the establishment, even if these changes have been battle tested in real life and have produced far better overall results, the deviation from the medical professions processes are being derided, rather than applauded. It appears that long time accepted practices are like a worn in shoe and contemplating a change, even for the better, is viewed like trying to turn a supertanker on a dime.

An actual experience makes the point. In a discussion with a nurse, it was her contention that a sole caretaker would not be able to turn a patient in bed and do wound care on the back at the same time. When asked why, the answer was that here at the hospital we have at least two people working on the patient, one doing the wound care, the other one holding the patient in place. My response was, "I don't see a ceiling lift over the bed!"

The nurse closed with, "Oh, is that what you use?" This is typical. The famous quote, "we always have done it this way," therefore it has to be the right way, is still very much the case.

By exposing some of these issues, hopefully you will be able to be a better advocate for your patient.

I hope you found the real life experiences, which resulted in the writing of this book, very beneficial. While entertaining it is primarily educational.

GOOD LUCK and GOD BLESS!

Appendix A

One couple's journey of love

A Manatee County man's devotion to his wife seems limitless

By Billy Cox

Published: Sunday, December 20, 2009 at 1:00 a.m.

When their fears were confirmed and Phyllis DeSoti was given a diagnosis in 1980 of progressive multiple sclerosis, husband Oliver knew what he had to do. Banking memories was at the top of the list.

They had always enjoyed traveling, at home and abroad. Now, there would be no "golden years" retirement adventures in their future. In 1982, they started taking trips around the world. By 1984, their quest to visit every state in the union was on.

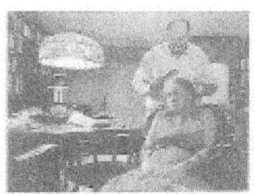

STAFF PHOTOS / DAN WAGNER
Oliver DeSoti gets his wife, Phyllis, ready to go out for dinner. Oliver is now a full-time caregiver for Phyllis, who is paralyzed by multiple sclerosis.

Phyllis was still ambulatory then; the worst was years away. When they moved to Manatee County in 1983, Oliver built a house for the day her feet would surrender to wheels.

Her deterioration descended as anticipated, in slow but decisive movements. She lost her mobility in 1992. The next year she lost her bladder control. By 2005 she was unable to speak. But every setback provoked a countermove, each designed to keep Phyllis from relaying the message Oliver knows would crush him: "I want to die."

So here's the scene today, inside a home where the temperature is always 82 degrees and the humidity hovers at a comfortable 50 percent.

Phyllis is 67 years old, weighs 90 pounds, and is paralyzed. Neither her nurse nor her neurologist have ever seen her with a bedsore. Her bed faces a big-screen TV, but just as important are the surveillance monitors allowing her to see outside. Oliver wired each door

OLIVER J. DESOFI

and window to an audio motion-sensor that announces all movement in the house.

Oliver is 79 and trying to keep the weight off. After a heart attack in 2008 informed him he needed to make more adjustments, he installed a portable electric ceiling lift to hoist her out of bed without strain. He put a 24-hour camera in the bedroom to review recordings of his own home-care performance, just in case something goes wrong.

Things can always go wrong. That's why Oliver bought a backup generator. And the inflatable boat in the garage, in case all hell breaks loose.

But the six hours or so he spends grooming her each day, feeding her, medicating her, checking her urine for infection — those are checklists for survival, not living.

"I remember when my dad called me from the airport one day and he said 'Listen, I'm recording planes taking off,'" said their daughter, Kerri Hansen. "I said, 'You're doing what? Why?'"

Because her mom and dad still take flights of fantasy, which are incomplete without sound effects.

When the Desofis travel today, it starts with the boarding passes Oliver saved from years ago. He narrates their way through security and pre-flight announcements.

With jet engines whirring in the background, he pulls out the menus from their trans-Atlantic journeys and serves up typical fare he prepared himself: a glass of champagne, maybe, smoked salmon with capers, onions, sour cream and sliced hard-boiled egg on rye bread. Coffee ice cream for dessert. And a James Bond movie or two. With touchdown in a photo album from familiar alien lands.

Sometimes Oliver can understand what she's saying. It never varies.

"I love these trips," she tells him, "because the food is delicious, we're always on time and we never crash."

Long love affair

Phyllis knocked his socks off the first time he laid eyes on her. That was in 1960. He was a bigwig at American Airlines in New York, charged with implementing a revolutionary computer-booking system called Sabre. She was interviewing for a secretarial job at 19. Among other things, she wore a hat, high heels and a pair of white gloves.

146

"I thought: Wow, I sure hope they hire her!" Oliver recalls.

He had two kids and a wife. She had a boyfriend. Some things can't be helped. They got free and got married in 1970.

Both were hunters, physically active, engaged by the outdoors. He never understood how she could so accurately read the distorting refraction of water to nail a fish with a bow and arrow. She liked to snow ski, even though she tended to lose her balance and fall a lot.

"I was maybe 3, 4 years old," says Kerri, their only child, remembering the first time she noticed something was wrong. "I was on the back of my dad's bicycle. Mom was having trouble and she fell off her bike. But she would never admit she had a problem. She's very stubborn. I think that's why she's still here today."

'Oliver lives for Phyllis'

The expressive eyes on Phyllis' unlined face widen when Oliver leans over and introduces her to a stranger. She approximates a smile and issues a one-note greeting reminiscent of a bow crawling across mid-range of a string instrument.

Oliver seeks her approval to have a photographer accompany them on their next monthly restaurant outing. He takes her hand. "It takes me four hours to get her ready," he says. "But when I'm done with her, she looks like a million bucks."

Oliver isn't joking when he calls Phyllis "my research project." He is conversant in the jargon of neurologists, nurses, and gastroenterologists. His comprehension of his wife's needs has graduated from informed to intuitive. And he has a goal, probably unrealistic, but one worth shooting for. He wants to erase the infection around the port of the feeding tube in her stomach.

This is a long story, involving a medical mishap and a personal-injury attorney who declined to take a winnable case due to prohibitive litigation costs. It left Phyllis with a 6-by-6-inch burn wound from stomach acids that "looked like you had applied a torch to it."

Since he began managing that injury from February 2008, Oliver has rolled back the inflammation to the diameter of a quarter. Part of the price for his fastidious vigil was a heart attack in March of last year. He would gladly lighten up if he could. But this is the truth, and everyone knows it: "Nobody," he says, "can care for her better than I can."

Carol Latto, a BayCare nurse with 40 years of experience, has been dropping in on Phyllis and Oliver for nearly two years. She comes once a week and stays an hour or so. Latto struggles to recall parallels.

"I've learned more from Oliver than he's learned from me," she says. "He's setting unrealistic expectations or goals for all of us. We can't all do this — we can't be something we're not. But this is who Oliver is. He's very patient with her. She loves hearing him read to her. I watch them talking to each other. Oliver lives for Phyllis."

At American Airlines, Oliver counted 120 employees working for him. As a top executive at National Westminster Bank, there were 1,400. Among the keys to his success were organizational skills, checklists, clockwork schedules. Latto has seen those same management standards at work in the DeSofi household. As has Dr. Dean Sutherland.

Sutherland is a neurologist at Sarasota Memorial Hospital; Phyllis has been his client for the past six or seven years. Sutherland speaks with Oliver almost as a professional peer.

"Most of what he's accomplished with Phyllis, he's done on his own," Sutherland says. "He comes in with these lists and says, 'OK, this isn't working, why don't we try this?' And most of the time, he's right. He's an amazing guy. I think he sees Phyllis as a problem he can figure out."

Like Latto, Sutherland knows all about the marriage-splintering tensions between MS patients and their spouses. He tries not to judge.

"But you promise to be together in sickness and in health," he says. "Your job is not to mourn the loss of who they were, but to embrace the person they are now. To do that, and maintain such a positive attitude, the way Oliver does — this is extremely unusual."

Surmounting obstacles

Oliver was born in Cuba to European parents. His mother moved to Germany and took him with her when he was 4. He attended a military academy during the Nazi era. The lies and propaganda he endured taught him the necessity of conducting his own research. The discipline demanded by that experience forced him into action.

"What I learned was, there is no obstacle you can't overcome," he says.

Consequently, the DeSofis have a treasury of memories to help them escape. They fell just three states shy — North Dakota, Oregon and Alaska — of visiting the entire country.

"We always had nice, long talks," Oliver remembers. "We never listened to the radio. We liked to talk. Or maybe listen to books on tape. We were always learning something. It sort of laid the foundation for where we are today."

As Christmas approaches, daughter Kerri says the foundation her parents laid makes the season seem like a speed bump.

"For some reason," says Kerri, who lives in Myakka City, "people tend to reach out or rethink things around the holidays. My parents taught me to live for today, to love for today. Because we really don't know what's going to happen tomorrow. They celebrate Christmas year-round.

"Dad's very impatient. If he sees a dress, he'll just buy it and say, 'Well, this is for Christmas 2023.' I got this gift for my husband Mike. Dad said 'Why don't you give it to him now? Why wait?'"

Oliver says their savings have been exhausted. Yet, the couple that refused to wait for the inevitable can — and does — travel around the world today. After all, the cornerstone of life with Phyllis is its simplicity.

Says Oliver, "I fell very much in love with her."

Appendix B

Living with and caring for people afflicted with severe disabilities. As seen from a Caregiver's perspective. (45 minute speech)

Good morning (afternoon), we, my wife Phyllis [*pointing to Phyllis who is sitting in her power wheelchair close to the podium*] and I appreciate the opportunity to address this wonderful audience.

Why **am I** standing before you to talk about disabled people like my wife who has Multiple Sclerosis? I haven't taken any courses in nursing, I am not a doctor and certainly not a neurologist, I don't even have a stethoscope around my neck. What can I possibly share with you in regard to this and other diseases?

I am a former corporate CEO, a professional people manager and a computer expert. When I reached the peak of my career I decided to retire early from my job as a Corporate CEO. I then answered an employment ad and accepted a promotion to Caregiver. Following is the ad and I quote: "*NEED IMMEDIATELY. CAREGIVER. Private home looking for that special person – keeping loads of records, lots of diversified work and a sense of humor. Never a minute of boredom – long hours, very low pay, no benefits, no coffee breaks, short lunch, no vacations, no bonuses, no raises, willing to work in a messy house and able to take much abuse. Love required!*" My MS afflicted wife hired me on the spot.

Training began immediately. As I became totally immersed in this new venture, the learning experience was immense. During that period, I had many conversations with other caregivers who encouraged me to document the many new tricks of this trade and share it with as many people as possible. This then prompted me to write a book which I titled "Caregiving–My Story–Your Guide." It is in the process of being published and should be available soon. Does that brief description of my background make me an expert? You will have a chance to decide!

So let us now concentrate on the real hero, my wife Phyllis. Please remember throughout this speech, that while my experiences as a caregiver relate to my wife and Multiple Sclerosis, they can also relate to caregivers of loved ones with many other diseases or accident victims and our wounded veterans returning from a war zone. Let's first take a look at the standard medical explanation for MS.

Multiple Sclerosis is a disease that destroys myelin, an insulating material that covers the nerve fibers and is necessary for the normal electrical function of the nervous system. As a result, an electrical short circuit develops, and normal electrical impulses cannot be carried by the nerves. The type of symptoms that result depends on where in the brain and spinal cord this process takes place, but usually, multiple sites are involved. Myelin has some ability to repair itself, but with repeated attacks of inflammation, scarring (sclerosis) takes place and permanent loss of function may result.

Because almost any area of the brain and spinal cord that contains myelin may be affected, the symptoms are very diverse, including but not limited to the appearance of a disabling event and then its disappearance. As the disease progresses, remission of symptoms between attacks becomes less and less complete.

It is not possible to provide a typical picture of Multiple Sclerosis. Some of the common symptoms, however, include loss of vision in one eye, double vision, loss of coordination, and trembling of a hand, instability in walking, spasticity, loss of bladder control, and peculiar spontaneous sensations such as a pins-and-needles feeling over part of the body. At first, the patient may have only intermittent symptoms. Since the physical examination at this stage may be completely normal, the patient's complaints may be dismissed initially as "psychosomatic" or "hysterical."

The descriptions of the **many other diseases** are portrayed in a similar fashion. It lists additional symptoms such as fatigue, weakness, difficulty speaking, breathing, swallowing and clumsiness which may manifest itself by not being able to perform precise tasks with your hands. They invariably detail a number of "unpleasant" surprises, in some cases followed by the most devastating statement of "THERE IS NO CURE," which has the "Oh, my God" impact. The fact remains that the list of symptoms doesn't necessarily mean that a person diagnosed with any one of these symptoms will get them all. There is a high probability some of those mentioned earlier, may never show up. Should you encounter them, the chances are it will be much later in life, hopefully when you are already retired. You know, some of the symptoms attributed to MS, such as loss of coordination, trembling of a hand, instability in walking and loss of bladder control may even show up without MS or any other ailment, it's just part of the aging process. THE PATIENT SHOULD NOT OVER REACT, GET SPOOKED OR FOCUS ON THE NEGATIVE. If you have one of these different ailments, but especially MS, you are probably thinking right now, "Hey, that's easy for you to say, you don't have MS!" Yes, it is easy to say. I am so intensely tuned in, that when my wife Phyllis describes different feelings, sometimes I get the symptoms as if my brain decides to give me a physical demonstration, it is bizarre. I am not making it up, it is the absolute truth.

Coming back to my earlier question; am I an expert and qualified to talk about the plight of disabled people or MS? The answer is yes because I am an experienced people manager. Managing a person afflicted with **MS or any other disease,** requires the psychological insight of a good professional manager. Now-a-days, true professional managers are hard to find. If you work for one, you are fortunate. You will recognize them immediately. Managing a diverse group of people successfully is no different than managing a person with a disease, especially one as varied in its medical expressions as MS. After I was accepted for the caregiver job, I got my PHD when I married my wife, Phyllis H. DeSofi. Who's initials are PHD. What impressed me about my wife was her perfect perception of the world around her. When her doctor finally diagnosed her disease he prescribed a medication. After she had it filled and viewed the bottle she had a panic attack. She called the doctor's office and asked, "Is it true that the medication you prescribed has to be taken for the rest of my life?" The doctor replied, "Yes, I'm afraid so." After she had absorbed his response, she then asked, "How serious is this disease called MS?" The doctor then said, "Why are you asking, I thought I had explained everything" which then prompted my wife to ask the 64,000 dollar question – "how come the bottle is marked NO REFILLS?" This and many non-curable diseases can instill quite some fear which has to be overcome.

In my description of experiences, I will concentrate on MS, but many of the issues have the same impact on disabled people, those suffering from a large number of other diseases or ailments. For many years now, to be exact, 44 years, I have been closely associated with the disease called MS. I am here to talk to you about this disease from a caregiver's perspective. My beautiful wife, Phyllis was finally diagnosed with MS in 1980, in spite of the fact that she had been suffering with many of the symptoms for 19 years before the year of diagnosis. During that period, she saw many neurologists and invariably got a diagnosis of "It's all in your head!" Unfortunately or maybe fortunately, MRI's didn't exist yet to determine how true that statement actually was. As you may know, MRI's basically display an image of your brain, showing the scaring created by MS, thus the expression "it's all in your head" is quite accurate. I give a lot of credit to the old time neurologists, unbeknown to them; they said the right thing but didn't know what it really meant.

While some of you are already counting off the years on your fingers since the onset of her MS, let me spare you the mathematical effort. As she sits there with her beaming smile, she has had MS for a total of 49 years. Some of you may say "WOW – she looks so good!" Actually she hates that expression, especially after she applied for disability benefits and her attorney said, "You look too good, they will give you a hard time." I am not going to repeat the response she delivered to the attorney. I think his ears are still ringing today!

She is about the most beautiful, courageous and determined person I have ever met. In spite of the fact that Phyllis looks good, we defied the odds and finally succeeded in federal court to get her disability approved. She is an inspiration to anybody associated with her. This disabled lady has given me strength and equally shares in our success to cope. Forty years ago we vowed to share our life until death do us part in sickness and in health and with every passing day I love her more despite the turbulence we have flown through.

There is no question that dealing with many of these diseases is a real challenge. If handled in a positive fashion, it can and will result in a long and still rewarding life for both. A life which will never prompt the patient to mutter the dreaded sentence, "I wish I were dead!"

Multiple Sclerosis as well as many other diseases not specifically mentioned should be viewed as a major nuisance. One can work around a nuisance and overcome it, thus changing the afflicted person's mindset from negative to positive.

As I said, I am a professional manager but I am also a computer specialist. My autobiography titled **"Intrigue, Capitalism, Love – My True Story"** was published in 2009. It describes a life which prompted some people to say, "You covered more ground in ten years than most will not cover in a lifetime." It is a story describing the true "American Dream." Because of my past I have a habit of dissecting everything to the nth degree. I have read many stories about experiences, observations and different views by a large variety of MS afflicted people. I have studied dissertations by experts and I have read the analysis by drug companies. A number of drug treatment plans allegedly produce certain positive results however the side effects they may cause, sometimes seem to be worse than the disease they are supposed to help or improve.

Over time, I have learned to analyze everything from many angles and you can too. I don't accept anything as a given. I keep an open mind and do not discard any approach which could potentially improve my wife's life style. I also believe, for any disease there is a cure or answer and in order to find it, we cannot close our minds to anything.

I am going to make some statements which are not intended to convey any other meaning than to prompt you to think about potential hidden motives.

Pharmaceutical companies managed to have Congress write into law that Medicare cannot negotiate discounted prices for your medication as part of Medicare Part D. Many severely disabled patients face medication costs which will choke a mule. Are you really going to believe that the drug companies have your best interests at heart when they portray drug treatments to you as being the solution for your problems? Maybe I am the only one who wonders if they are motivated by the almighty dollar and want to enrich themselves rather than making sure your life will be more rewarding. Based on our experience, I even wonder if some of the treatment plans actually produce the stated favorable results? For some they may, for others they will not. Think about it! Staying away from certain expensive mediations should be considered as a viable option.

It's not only drug companies who attempt to rake you over the coals. There are many so called "well meaning" people out there who have found that miracle cure, people who stopped taking the drugs and used their alleged alternative "cure." They will not tell you what the cure consists of, such as what weed or pill has produced that favorable reaction. They just dedicate much language explaining why they are prevented from opening up on the internet, but they certainly have no inhibition to sell you their miracle drug over the same internet. Am I a cynic? I get the impression they just want to make a fast buck and take advantage of your disability by telling you what you really would like to hear, the word we all love, "A CURE!" I find a lot of them as I roam around the internet. Some of those stories should have a warning label, "Only for suckers!" Don't be tempted, there is a high probability that you will not be happy after the purchase.

Another issue I see no coverage about. Maybe I missed it. In an advanced state, MS patients can be as unprotected as a baby. Let's face reality, the reason MS affected people or for that matter any disabled person encounter many outside obstacles is plain and simple. The majority of the people don't care, some are actually cruel, and some are just plain greed driven. Don't waste your time to change them! Ignore them! Do what is right for you!

Some of the articles I read in MS related literature concentrate on the fact that more education is necessary. I say, that is putting it mildly. What we need is a wake up call, maybe a 2 by 4 to help people along! MS afflicted people are more prone to be abandoned by their own spouse, the person who made a vow of "till death do us part" and we are led to believe that we can just "educate" the other people and make them understand. What are they thinking? Where is the logic? Political correctness is a form of education! As a society we have managed to rename the "mailman" now called the "mail person." Those that didn't know how to spell "mail" decided to call it the "person-person" job. Did that educational effort toward correctness change the delivery of your mail? I don't think so!

When we turn the TV on or you sign on to the internet, we are bombarded with commercials, hype, distortions, news clips and many special shows which are nothing more than outright propaganda. You are given standard versions of what is good and bad. Who is the judge? Repeat things enough and you will accept it as a fact and the truth. How about just THE PLAIN TRUTH, wouldn't that be refreshing? Don't accept anything as a given! Question everything and everyone!

The mindset of the patient and their caregiver is the best weapon by far to "defying the odds!"

Think about it! Who cares what other people understand or don't understand about MS. Who cares what they do or not do?

Let's face it! Nerve related diseases are unique to a patient, they are basically singular diseases. No two people have the same disease, they just can't. It depends on how the vast nervous system has been affected, impaired or damaged. Who knows the disease best? The affected person! They know it better than all the medical professionals, your neighbors, co-workers or any other person crossing your path. Don't let the disease be an inhibitor for anything and if at all possible, only confide into a very small circle of people. If you extend the circle, the many misconceptions, false impressions and plain stupidity by the public at large will cause you unnecessary grief. It also opens a door for some very costly additional grief, specifically Insurance coverage! If you currently have health insurance, you are lucky. Will it last? Will it follow you? Will you or your spouse be fortunate enough to work for an organization which will provide affordable health insurance even if you have a pre-existing condition? The answer has to be "MAYBE!"

For the new comers to the MS world, if you have any symptoms as those I mentioned earlier and you want to see a neurologist just to find out what your problem may be, pay him cash. If the neurologist feels you should have a MRI evaluation, pay cash. Do not use your insurance. MRI's are expensive, but you can negotiate them down if you pay cash. Would you believe you can negotiate a 74% discount, YES YOU CAN!

If you pay cash for your visit to the neurologist and for your MRI, should you be diagnosed with MS, I can guarantee you that you will more than offset future expenses. The doctor is under no obligation to report the results. If you use your insurance you will be a marked person. I will put it mildly. Being a marked person when it comes to insurance really translates into grief – lots of grief!

Once you are diagnosed, depending at what stage it occurs, don't be fooled by the traditional concept that early detection will allow you to attack the disease in its beginning stages, thus improving your longevity. The description of MS clearly states that there is currently no cure. If you have been diagnosed, as cold as it might sound, in order to overcome, you have to first accept it. The good news is that MS is not a leading cause of death. Some MS patients can live a relatively comfortable life even by not taking any more medication than the people around you **without** MS.

Keeping the circle of those that must know about your condition to a small group of people is extremely important. Don't complain about strange symptoms and don't let anybody focus on it; try to keep it private as long as possible. Isn't that in conflict with what I just said regarding truth? There is a big difference between keeping things private and not being open about your medical condition. You will be treated like the child who is taught to always be honest, no matter what. This young fellow took his parents at their word and one day announced he accidentally dropped his mother's beautiful Ming Dynasty vase and shattered it into a thousand pieces. For his honesty he wasn't praised, he was smacked. If you are too open about your condition, you will be smacked; you will pay dearly for not keeping things private.

We have dealt with this disease now for many years, but since it is such a unique disease, I cannot stand here and tell you what has worked for us would produce the same or similar results for you, maybe yes, maybe not. All I can assure you is that if you spend some time and effort analyzing everything, question everything and trust your instincts, you will find the best path for you.

My main purpose is to encourage you to become an independent thinker. A variety of sources can give you ideas as to what may or may not work for you. In the end, you must lay out a course that is best for you and do it with conviction.

Our joint attitude is that obstacles are there to be overcome, the larger the obstacles, the greater the rewards. As we experienced the downward progression of Phyllis' MS, we never gave up. Phyllis' severity is rated a 9 on a scale of 1 (good) to 10 (really bad), however our joint attitude remained stuck at one. We are very grateful because there are many people out there who have more severe problems than us. {Pause} Let's now change the subject.

I am now going to give you two examples; one which shows a tumble because I was under the misguided belief that a professional medical person paid attention and the other as to how a totally disabled person can, for a few hours, forget his or her disability. Both of these examples are true.

Example 1: Phyllis has been permanently in a wheelchair since 1992. Sometimes people ask me why she is in a wheelchair followed by the statement she hates the most "she looks so good." My inclination is to say, she is too damned lazy to walk, but I am polite and say, she has a problem and can't walk. She cannot control anything, not even the wheelchair. She has had a catheter for longer than anyone else, at least at this particular Urology Treatment Center. The standard rule is that catheters should be changed once a month, at least the insurance companies feel that is reasonable. Clogging of the catheter started to become a problem in what I will call **MONTH ONE**. The first reaction was, have you flushed the catheter? PLACE THE BLAME ON THE CAREGIVER FIRST. It was made crystal clear that it had nothing to do with flushing, because it could be flushed and one hour later it was clogged like a cork had been placed on the other end. The first replacement was with another catheter of the same size, just earlier. This condition started to repeat itself and the answer was to increase the size of the catheter until the only thing left was a garden hose. Other problems showed up and the experts didn't come up with anything to reverse the trend, except that an operation was recommended in order to have the catheter inserted into the bladder through her belly rather than having it inserted through the urethra.

Here again I started to ask for explanations. The reason and rationale for the operation is based on the fact that "debris" from the bladder has a tendency to clog the catheter. Could it clog even if inserted through the belly? Of course it can, but it is less likely. How less likely? That is hard to say! The truth is, they don't have a clue.

By month five, Phyllis' eating started to become a problem and she started to get weaker. In month six, she had a severe attack and 104.5 fever. She was almost paralyzed and rushed to the emergency room. She was diagnosed with a severe kidney infection while her pancreas and liver gave signs of wanting to shut down. Nothing was ever done to find the cause of this mudslide, basically the debris which clogged the catheter repeatedly.

The doctor was not as hopeful as I would have wanted for him to be, but he still was determined to help her through to recovery.

A drainage line was inserted into her right kidney. A PIC line was inserted into her left arm for antibiotics and because she was unable to eat, a tube was inserted into her stomach. They had found a golf ball size kidney stone, a stone in her bladder and the infection was severe. She was in the Intensive Care Unit (ICU) and for six days Phyllis was in a semi coma, rarely opening her eyes and not being aware of anything. That sixth night, a family member was on guard duty. I left the hospital at eleven o'clock. At two in the morning I received a call to come to the hospital because Phyllis was asking for me. I went immediately and when I arrived, she took my hand and asked me, "What am I doing here?" I started to explain when she interrupted me and said, "Get me out of here!" It was then that I finally knew, I would have my honey back.

I prayed and prayed, while still in critical condition, she suddenly showed some key improvements. Her right kidney showed a revival, something that surprised even the doctor. Without a doubt, the almighty answered my prayers and gave her a helping hand. On day nine, a Friday, still in ICU, I was informed that she would be released. I looked at the doctor and at Phyllis in disbelief. Here is a patient with a drainage tube coming out of her right kidney, a catheter in her urethra, a line into her vein to give her antibiotics twice a day, a feeding tube in her stomach and an oxygen tube in her nose. In addition to that the nurses tested her glucose level several times a day, gave her insulin shots to bring her glucose readings to an acceptable range and her urine had to be checked for any unusual signs, like blood and the degree of clarity. Now they want to release her into my care, when I have to push all these tubes away, just to give her a kiss. Then a nurse told me that insurance companies don't like to pay hospital expenses if they can UNLOAD the patient. They put a lot of pressure on doctors. I told my doctor, the only way I will accept a release is if all the doctors involved and there were four, answer all the questions which I will give to them in writing. I immediately sat down and listed all my questions; I came up with a total of 42 questions, covering issues such as **WHAT TO DO, HOW TO DO IT and WHAT**

TO WATCH OUT FOR. I made one sheet for each doctor. The nurses got on the phone to each doctor and obtained the answers I needed.

By two in the afternoon, I had them and I accepted the release. I was overwhelmed and the homecare help I received was bare bones. I entered everything into the computer playing data entry clerk while paying attention to Phyllis. Eventually I compiled my schedule with an hourly description of all the tasks to be done and the numerical data I had to check or maintain, including her blood pressure, temperature and glucose level. It went from 7AM to 11PM each and every day for a 17 day period, non-stop, when the PIC line came out of her vein. The drainage line from her kidney didn't come out until after she had an operation to remove the kidney stone, which occurred 30 days after her release from the hospital. 30 days after that, she was scheduled for another operation when they removed the bladder stone.

While I was overwhelmed when she was released into my care, I am now thankful that they forced me into this situation. I seriously doubt that she would have gotten anywhere near the very detailed and minute by minute attention in the hospital. You may say now that you could never do what I did. I would have thought the same. However when the situation presents itself so does the strength.

My biggest reward is when she expresses her deep appreciation for all I do and that there is no way she would feel at all happy and comfortable without my help. I am not good at handling praise so my response is, "You are just a pain, I have no choice to do what I am doing" and she retorts with her favorite response, "Jerk!" She smiles at me, we both laugh and I kiss her.

By now you must feel, enough is enough, what else could she have? Well, her voice chords are affected and sometimes she thinks she is talking, while moving her lips yet nothing comes out. If you happen to call her at that time, you would have a hard time knowing what she is trying to say unless you have one of those camera phones and you can read her lips, provided she doesn't hold the camera to her ear, so that she can hear you better.

Now that I have given you a synopsis of Phyllis' MS, all I can say, unfortunately, at this point, a reversal of the MS disease is not in the cards. The future is full of expectations and hope. She hopes that one of these days the researchers follow in the steps of the highway engineers.

I am sure you have seen "runaway ramps" for vehicles with failed brakes on steep downward slopes to give them a chance to recover from certain destruction. After the vehicle has stopped, it can then be inspected to determine why the brakes failed. Hopefully MS researchers can find an inhibitor to the myelin destruction entity, be it a gene, a virus or some other problem and in time figure out what causes MS. Phyllis' biggest asset is the fact that she is a strong-willed person, who will still tell me what, how and when to do whatever her fabulous brain can invent.

Nowadays, Phyllis is mostly bed-ridden and generally tube fed. All her medications are crushed and fed through the tube. She has to eat easy to swallow items in order to exercise her throat muscles. Her ability to speak is greatly inhibited because she doesn't have sufficient power to push air through her vocal chords. There are a number of other medical requirements which have to be attended to. This may sound pretty depressing if you are inclined to give up. I am a strong believer in "positive thinking." A person with a positive attitude will have the power to overcome many apparent insurmountable obstacles. In light of this, I feel it is important that this "ATTITUDE TO OVERCOME" remains a very high priority.

Now for Example 2 the fantasy trip: The next issue covers an event which will demonstrate that with a little bit of imagination one can make a totally disabled person feel like a million bucks.

Before it became more difficult for Phyllis to travel by plane, we traveled extensively. So from time to time, Phyllis and I embark on another one of our trips only this is an imaginary escapade. After she woke up from a deep sleep I attended to all the chores necessary to make her bed-rest as comfortable as possible. I decided it was time to surprise her and embark on one of the many beautiful trips of earlier times. I picked a memorable international trip, one of our flights on a Boeing 747 from London to New York. I picked this event because it had a lot of memory attached. We all have some memorable events in our lives like your honeymoon, special shopping trips, a wonderful vacation by plane or by car, the day your child or grand child was born and many other experiences. The fact that I selected this particular event doesn't mean you can't let your imagination go wild and convert whatever memorable and enjoyable experience you may have encountered along your life path into action.

I set the stage by reminding her of the time when we came from Saudi Arabia and stayed in London several days in order to visit with friends before returning to the US. We had stayed at the London Hilton and the day we were checking out of the hotel it took forever and I had been whispering wise remarks into Phyllis' ears. She started to laugh and when we turned around and looked at the people behind us, we both starting laughing because their facial expressions clearly said, "what's the matter with these dumb Americans – what's so funny." After I had brought that memory back, she started laughing again.

I inserted a cassette that I made into our tape recorder. It was a recording of jets taking off and landing at an airport. This created the appropriate atmosphere as we are arriving at Heathrow airport in the beginning of our make believe trip. I now started to talk like I was reading a bedtime story.

Hey Phyllis, here we are, we just arrived at the departure area. The skycap is opening the door to the cab and helps you out. I am getting out of the cab from the other side. The driver is handing the 3 pieces of luggage to the skycap who places them on his trolley to move them into the terminal. After I paid the taxi driver we follow the skycap. As we arrive at the counter, the skycap places the luggage at our feet and looked at us. To make things look more real for Phyllis, I pulled a British ten pound note from my pocket like I was giving the skycap his tip but I showed it to Phyllis and then put it back into my other pocket. She smiled at me. We are now standing in line holding our passports and tickets when one of the American Airlines employees comes up to us and asks "did you pack your own bags?" I look at Phyllis and ask her "did you pack all the junk you bought at Portobello Road, the famous antiques market in London." Phyllis starts laughing and said, "boy; you keep on rubbing it in, I love those copper pots." Well, I now look away and make believe I am talking to the American Airlines employee and answer "YES."

The line is moving and we are being welcomed by the ticket agent who looks at our passports, takes our tickets and eventually hands us our boarding passes and baggage tags. We now proceed through the various government checkpoints, getting our passports inspected again and being asked more questions. After going through that exercise we are now standing in line all over again. Finally we are beginning to move toward the gate and approach the dreaded security check point. This time we will not have to strip to our underwear or have the agent brush us with his wand that beeps if we had an iron rich apple a few minutes prior. Fortunately those new machines that look right through you to determine if you digested your pancake have not entered our fantasy world yet. The imaginary boarding process is so much more efficient and safe. I look at Phyllis and say, "I am ready for a drink, are you and she nods wildly and laughs."

There is the announcement, flight 123 to New York is now ready for boarding, all disabled and handicap passengers please board first. We will then board first class passengers and after that we board by rows. We proceed toward the plane, make a left turn and move to the first two seats at the front of the plane. We are now ready for our glass of Champaign. Hidden behind me I had a bottle of Champaign. I poured some into a tiny cup and using a straw, dropped a little bit into her mouth. While I had been talking, the tape recorder was playing the jet noise at a low sound setting,

Pretty soon the door is closed and the plane is pushed back. Now the jet engines start up and I now increase the volume to simulate the noise of our own aircraft's jet engines. Soon the plane is moving faster and faster down the runway and we are climbing toward cruising altitude. I now make belief that I am the Captain and welcome us all on board of American Airlines flight 123 to New York. Ladies and Gentlemen, this is my first transatlantic flight and I hope I will find the new world, especially New York. Phyllis looks at me and laughs and honors me with her favorite word "Jerk." Now I start to tube feed her some nutritional supplement and ask here to close her eyes and imagine that she is having her favorite hors de oeuvres, smoked salmon pieces with onion bits, capers, minced hard boiled eggs and sour cream served with cocktail sized rye bread slices, while sipping at a cooled glass of delicious white wine of a quality the airline executives looking for that extra penny in profits wouldn't want to serve. She opens her eyes and said, "You wish!" I now turn the tape recorder off and place one of her favorite movies, a "007 James Bond" episode, into the DVD player in order to watch our in flight movie. While she is watching, I refill my glass with Champaign and we now enjoy our movie. After the movie is over, I remind her about the fabulous meal we were served on that flight. The stewardess was pushing her cart loaded with delicious entrées down the aisle. We both picked a succulent dinner composed of small pieces of chateaubriand, mashed potatoes and carrots, followed by a piece of mocha torte and a cup of coffee.

Phyllis said, "Wouldn't that be great?" It certainly would beat the monotony of my tube feeding routine, but at least we had that experience, that in itself is worth it.

Pretty soon we disembark from our imaginary trip and I welcome Phyllis to New York. I assured her that on this particular trip we are certain our three pieces of luggage will not end up in Rio, Honolulu and Johannesburg, as on one of the real trips. As a matter of fact, it will not get lost at all. The customs officials at Kennedy airport will not grill us, as they did on our real trip, regarding the "Cans of Danish Ham" in our luggage. They lectured us regarding food items that cannot be brought into the country, in spite of the fact that all you see at your supermarket is imported food. Well Phyllis did you enjoy another one of our spectacular trips? She responds with a broad smile and tells me, "I love these trips, they are better than the real ones. We don't ever run into delays and we certainly always make it back safe and sound. I love you!"

Can I ask for anything more rewarding?? You should try it!

In closing I am going to tell you the most important thing about being a sole caregiver or provider of care.

[Walk away from podium toward the exit, in essence abandoning Phyllis and then turn around and return to the podium]

You just don't walk away from someone you love!!!

Appendix C

TPN (Total Parenteral Nutrition) Process

Following are the specific steps which had to be followed every day in order to prepare and connect the TPN solution to the PIC line. When the nurse taught me the process, I decided to document all the steps in order to avoid any potential mistakes, since this was very critical. A misstep could have been dangerous to my wife and the loss of a bag for whatever reason would have had some severe financial consequences.

TPN PROCESS - PART I

Items required: Get
1. One syringe of Sodium Chloride
2. One 10ml 20G1 Syringe
3. One fresh tubing
4. Two "AA" batteries for pump
5. Vitamins - a.) BLUE cap vial and b.) WHITE cap vial
6. Insulin vial
7. Insulin syringe
8. Three alcohol swaps
9. Rubber gloves
10. Take bag out of refrigerator 1 and ½ hour before preparation.

WASH HANDS AND DRY WITH PAPER TOWELS

Preparation of Bag:
11. Pull separation strips from bag and discard
12. Mix contents of bag until evenly distributed. Beware of any sharp objects in order not to damage the bag
13. With Insulin syringe (Item 7) extract 30 units of Insulin (Item 6) by first disinfecting top of vial with alcohol swap (Item 8) then inject into bag. (BE CAREFUL NOT TO PUNCTURE THE BAG)
14. With 10ml syringe (Item 2) extract contents of BLUE cap vial (Item 5a) by first disinfecting top of vial with alcohol swap (Item 8) then extract contents of WHITE cap vial (Item 5b) by first disinfecting top of vial with alcohol swap (Item 8) then injecting the combined mixture into the bag.
15. Still using the syringe (Item 2) pull TPN mixture from bag and re-inject in order to push insulin further in.
16. Mix bag again in order to evenly spread the addition to the bag.
17. Remove the cap from the feeding tube nozzle and push the spike from the new tubing into the feeding tube nozzle. It requires some pressure to properly position the spike into the bag. Be careful and make sure it is totally locked in.
18. Hang bag up and let the TPN mixture fill the tubing. It can't exit because there is a cap at the end.

TPN PROCESS - PART 2

PUT ON RUBBER GLOVES (ITEM 5)

Installing TPN bag through Pump to Picline.

1. Turn PUMP off by pressing [STOP] then [OFF/ON]
2. Remove wrapping from sodium chloride syringe (Item 1).
3. Take alcohol swap out
4. Remove old tubing from picline and hold.
5. Disinfect end of picline
6. Remove cap from syringe (Item 1)
7. Connect syringe (Item 1) to picline and with a push/stop motion, inject about 3/4 of sodium chloride into the picline, remove syringe and cap the picline with the cap from the syringe.
8. NOW START THE WORK WITH THE PUMP

Getting the Pump ready

9. Disconnect old tubing and remove
10. Take old batteries out and replace them with 2 new "AA" batteries
11. Insert new tubing and make sure it is properly seated and is snapped in.
12. Press [ON/OFF] button
13. Pump will ask if you are on batteries. Press [YES/ENTER] to battery question
14. It will now ask if you want to resume. Press [1] for the proper choice
15. On the screen of the pump you will see on the right hand lower corner a "C"
16. Press [CHANGE] now
17. The screen will ask now if it is a new container
18. Press [1] to confirm
19. Press [PURGE] holding button until you see line filling to end
20. Now take cap off end of tubing, swap the picline connection and screw the new line firmly on.
21. Press [START]

Pump buttons
[Silence] [STOP] [START] [Power]
 [Screen]   [ON/OFF]
 [Screen]   [Back-up]
            ⟶ "C" [CHANGE]
                         [Options]
[PURGE] [Help] [No] [YES/ENTER]

Appendix D

SAMPLE OF MEDICAL CONTROL SHEET

Medical Control Sheet Date	Medication	Schedule	Name = 1 Name = 2 Name = 3											
01:00AM	87.5	80	13x72									A	B	C D E
07:35AM					200									
08:02AM		94		2							X			
01:25AM	96.8	100	145PM			350	63	X	X					
11:35PM						635	110	X					342.5	
01:30PM														
05:00PM		426		566	816			X						
06:00PM	97.4													
09:55PM		180	10x50	2										
08:70PM						600	190	X	X					
09:00PM														
10:00PM				225	170								150	
11:35PM	93					350	50	X	X					
1:00PM														
1:30PM	34.3	94	13x76											L

NOTES:
A-Pain in setting
B-IV storage changed
C-Feels tired
D-Nerve pain left side of face
E-Did vomit

Appendix E

RECORD OF DOCTOR'S VISIT

RECORD OF DOCTOR'S VISIT FOR

DATE:

Doctor's Name

Address

Reason for visit

Treatment prescribed

Your comments

Specialty

Tax deductible miles:

Tax deductible cost of visit

TOTAL RECORD OF PRESCRIPTIONS

Date	Medicine prescribed	Rx #	Pharmacy	Doctor	Tax deductible cost	miles

Appendix F

Oliver J DeSofi
5101 Estates Circle
Sarasota, FL 34243-4925
TEL. 941-355-5055
FAX 941-358-9594
e-mail: dsfi@aol.com

December 29, 2004

Ms. Robin W. Williams
Founder and Chairperson
MS Centers of Florida Foundation VIA FACSIMILE: 772-794-0084
1655 27th Street-Suite 1
Vero Beach, FL 32960-3384

Dear Ms. Williams:

Today, I received your letter including the contribution request dated December 22, 2004, addressed to my wife Phyllis DeSofi, a severely disabled MS patient. I read your letter with great interest and the description of the Foundation's purpose and mission is admirable, especially your point regarding the social services.

My wife is now 62 years young and has had MS for 43 years. She has been wheelchair bound for the 18 years. She has had to change her catheter every 4 weeks for the last 11 years. I have reached the mature age of 75 and am her only 24/7 caretaker. I can't afford to get sick and if I do, my responsibilities to this very dear patient do not disappear. Why am I telling you this?

In the past, I have asked the MS support group to hopefully assist me in two specific cases when I had a problem:

- Would it be possible to have a volunteer take my wife to the doctor? If necessary, the volunteer can use my "wheelchair transport" Van. The answer — NO!
- Can some person help me for two or three days with the caretaker responsibility while I recover from a medical procedure? The answer — NO!

Since then I have not asked for any assistance in spite of the fact that the progression of my wife's disease and the clock work against both of us.

If you could provide me with any information making the last sentence of the 3rd paragraph of your letter a reality – specifically "… make their (*MS patients*) lives a bit more comfortable, a bit more positive, a bit more productive…", I would be forever grateful.

In light of the above mentioned situation, I would love to be a "Sand Dollar" contributor, but I m not even in a position to qualify as an "Ocean Current" contributor, since more often than not, I spend more time under the "Ocean Current" than above.

Your kind attention to this information request would be appreciated.

Sincerely yours,

Oliver J. DeSofi

Appendix G

Oliver J. DeSofi
5101 Estates Circle
Sarasota, FL 34243
Tel.: 941-355-4994
January 21, 2010

Ms. Suzanne Mintz
President-NFCA Certified Letter
10400 Connecticut Ave. – Suite 500 7008 1830 0002 0360 1906
Kensington, MD 20895

Dear Ms Mintz:

Since I have written two letters to you before and never received a response, I decided to send this letter "Certified Mail." Obviously something happened that those previous letters did not end up in your "inbox."

I am a member of your organization and recently signed on to your website in search of an answer to a question and found your every day message, specifically

"**Believe** in yourself." I do!
"**Protect** your health." I do!
"**Reach** out for help." This letter is an attempt!
"**Speak** up for your rights." I am doing just that!

According to your goal and mission statement I found the following and I quote, "improve the overall quality of life of American Family caregivers" and "teach family caregivers more effective communications techniques to better advocate for the care recipients and themselves."

I am a 24/7 caregiver who is lacking some of these important skills and would like to receive your course on these techniques. I went to your on-line store and found an item labeled as:

"Improving Doctor/Caregiving Communications" (pack of 20)
Cost for members $ 6.00
Cost for non-members $ 9.00

What is meant by a "pack of 20?" I am not a school, I am an individual!

Furthermore, the descriptive break-out of this item talks about common sense issues like "Tips for Doctors from Family Caregivers" and "Tips from Family Caregivers for Doctors." Nowhere can I find the "educational material" teaching an individual the communications skills required to be a better advocate according to your mission statement.

I am trying to be as precise as possible so that you can understand what I am looking for. Thank you in advance for your kind response.

Sincerely yours,
Oliver J. DeSofi

Following is a response:

On February 19, I received a colorful and lengthy "DONATION" solicitation. Here are some of the highlights contained in this donation request.

I quote, *"We serve the needs of the family caregiver – enabling them to care for themselves and others to the best of their ability and honoring their devotion and service."*

Another quote, *"***WHAT DO** *family caregivers need? They need support, empowerment, encouragement to take care of themselves so that they may take better care of their loved ones. Family caregivers seek information, education and tools that can help them in managing the daunting tasks they face. They seek respite care, validation and an emotional outlet that will not burden their care recipient. They need the National Caregivers Association.*

Slick language but totally meaningless! There is not one item including "providing that emotional outlet" meaning your stories will find their way into print to be shared with others. I have provided information to test that concept but it received the same attention as all my previous letters.

Based on real life experiences by this 24 year caregiver veteran, the Telephone Directory and the Internet provide contact information. GOOGLE provides tools and education supplemented with input from the physician of the disabled patient. You will never receive a donation request from Internet providers or the different telephone directories.

You can reach your own conclusion !!!

Appendix H

The GOOGLE listing:

<u>MSAA – The Multiple Sclerosis Association Of America</u>
The official site of the **Multiple Sclerosis Association** of America. Our work is deeply
Rooted in care and understanding. Our message is one of hope.
<u>www.msassociation.org/</u>–Cached – Similar

<u>Programs & Services Publications</u>
<u>Contact MSAA Volunteer</u>
<u>Donate MSAA Calendar of Events</u>
<u>About Multiple Sclerosis Login</u>
<u>More results from msassociation.org ></u>

e-mails dictated by the MS patient:
Number 1
——Original Message—-
From: <u>dsfi@aol.com</u>
To: <u>webmaster@msassociation.org</u>
Sent: Thu, Jan. 28, 2010 1:13 pm
Subject: Easing Daily Life

I am 67 years old with primary-progressive MS and in a quadriplegic state. I currently have a hospital setting in my home but need to transfer to my daughter's home. In order to facilitate this move, I need temporarily a hospital bed at the new location until my current bed can be moved. Can your "Easing Daily Life" program help me and if yes, who would I have to contact? Your literature states and I quote "certain income requirements apply." What are the income requirements?

Your response would be greatly appreciated.
Dictated by Phyllis H. DeSofi
dsfi@aol.com

Number 2
From: dsfi@aol.com
To: webmaster@msassociation.org
Subject: Fwd: Easing Daily Life
Date: Sat, Feb. 6, 2010 11:43 am

On January 28, I sent you an e-mail asking you a question (attached). Do you just pretend that you help people with MS to collect donations? The courtesy of a response to my question regarding your alleged program "Easing Daily Live" would be a wonderful event!!!

Dictated by Phyllis H. DeSofi
dsfi@aol.com

Number 3
From: dsfi@aol.com
To: ctalbot@msassociation.org
Subject: Fwd: Easing Daily Life
Date: Mon, Feb.15, 2010 3:55 pm

On February 6, I e-mailed you a follow-up regarding a question I raised in my e-mail of January 28. Apparently your organization doesn't really mean what it states. If I wait long enough, I will not need what I asked for because I will be dead.

Is this what you call "our work is deeply rooted in care and understanding, our message is one of hope." I have been HOPING that this MS afflicted patient in a quadriplegic state would at least get the courtesy of a response to a very simple question. Is this too much to hope for? Did I set my goals too high?

Dictated by this frustrated MS suffering patient called Phyllis H. DeSofi
dsfi@aol.com

On February 17, 2010 they did respond with an apology. They confirmed that they had an equipment program unfortunately a hospital bed was not a part of the program. They suggested that the MS Society or MS Foundation may be able to assist in funding the purchase of a hospital bed. If not successful, they suggested to contact them again and they would do some research to see if other organizations could help. Then they provided Phyllis with a link to their equipment program.

Again, you can reach your own conclusion.

Appendix I

OBSERVATIONS-QUESTIONS-ANSWERS

While I was working on this book, the Health Care debate was in high gear. As a result of my work as a 24/7 caregiver and having encountered numerous problems with our health care system, I was very interested in the discussions which took place. I always felt civil discussions about issues of this magnitude are very valuable. There are many experiences that people have had over time and airing them in a give and take environment is important, besides it is our right as citizens of this great nation. What I listened to, day in and day out, was vitriolic comments, falsehoods, outright lies and distortions of gargantuan proportions.

We are a nation of people who go to the supermarket or card store and buy "Get Well Cards" with flowery or comical language to wish our family, friends, colleagues and neighbors well. Then you see these people at town hall meetings shouting down any person who just wants to ask a rational question or make a valued comment. I don't get it! God forbid we want to share and share alike! The verbal attacks on any person wanting to change the status quo are a show of incredible viciousness.

I feel any nation to be successful and powerful must be well educated (all its citizens), must have a superb health care system for all and must provide for the defense of its citizen. It is said, that we have the best universities, but why then do we import "educated" people from other countries on H1 visas and pay them slave labor salaries? Do our employers and corporations want educated people or cheap labor? It is also said that we have fine medical institutions, then why when it comes to our health care system for our citizens we are listed along with the third world countries rather than on top of the industrialized world?

These are just a few observations. Somehow our environment has changed drastically over the last 40 years, unfortunately not for the better. I could ask questions after questions, but it would really distract from the purpose of this book. Feel free to contact me through my website www.desofibook.com if you have any questions. I will do my very best to answer questions or comments.